T0191359

MONSTROUS MAMMALS

BY
JERRY PALLOTTA

ILLUSTRATED BY
ROB BOLSTER

SCHOLASTIC

The publisher would like to thank the following for their kind permission to use their photographs in this book: Photos ©: 8: Avalon.red/Alamy Stock Photo; 9: Thomas Mangelsen/Minden Pictures; 18: J & C Sohns/age fotostock; 19: slowmotiongli/Shutterstock; 22: Michel & Christine Denis-Huot/Biosphoto; 23: Anup Shah/Photodisc/Getty Images; 24: Avalon.red/Alamy Stock Photo; 25: Renee Lynn/Corbis/VCG/Getty Images; 42 bottom: Juniors/Superstock, Inc.; 43 bottom: Daniel J. Cox/Photographer's Choice/Getty Images; 44 top: Courtesy of Skulls Unlimited; 45 top: Courtesy of Skulls Unlimited; 46: Martin Zwick/age fotostock/Superstock, Inc.; 47: Victoria Stone & Mark Deeble/Getty Images; 52: Chokniti Khongchum/Shutterstock; 53: vovol/Shutterstock; 72: mikeuk/Getty Images; 73: Kevin Schafer/Getty Images; 77: Wolfgang Kaehler/LightRocket/Getty Images; 86: Sylvain Cordier/Gamma-Rapho/Getty Images; 87: John Eastcott and Yva Momatiuk/Getty Images; 104 top: tobkatrina/Getty Images; 104 bottom: tommy_martin/Getty Images; 105 top: Africa Studio/Shutterstock; 106 top: nater23/Getty Images; 107 top: taviphoto/Getty Images; 111 bottom: Courtesy the Perth Mint; 112 top: johnaudrey/Getty Images; 119 top: Deliris/Shutterstock.

Thank you to my research assistants, Olivia Packenham and Will Harney. Also, thank you to author and zoo guy Roland Smith.
To my pals Sean, Curran, and Marialice.
To my favorite banker, Ellen Gillette.
Welcome to the world, Reese Miller.

—J.P.

Thank you to M.C. Escher.
To my favorite beachgoers, Mark and Maureen.
To all dog lovers.

—R.B.

ISBN 978-1-5461-0993-8

10 9 8 7 6 5 4 3 2 1 24 25 26 27 28

Printed in China 38
This edition first printing, 2024
Cover design by Walter Chiu

TABLE OF CONTENTS

WHO WOULD WIN?™

What would happen if a lion and a tiger met each other? What if they were both hungry? What if these two big cats had a fight? Who do you think would win?

SCIENTIFIC NAME OF LION
"Panthera leo"

Meet the lion. Lions are mammals. Their fur is one solid color—tan, brown, or dark tan. They have no stripes or spots on their fur. Lions have an unforgettable face.

SCIENTIFIC NAME OF TIGER
"Panthera tigris"

DID YOU KNOW?

Lions and tigers look different on the outside. But inside they are similar. Both cats have excellent eyesight, hearing, and sense of smell.

Meet the tiger. Tigers are mammals too! Tigers are orange or rust-colored with black stripes. Underneath their soft fur is lots of muscle.

These two big cats live mostly on different continents. Almost all lions live in Africa. A few lions can be found in the Gir Forest of India, in Asia.

DID YOU KNOW?

A white tiger is a genetic mutant. Zoos love them because they attract more visitors than naturally colored tigers.

Tigers live in many parts of Asia. The largest tiger is the Siberian, or Amur, tiger.

Lions prefer to live on open, grassy plains.

Bonus Fact

A grassy plain is a perfect place for a lion to live. Lions mostly eat animals that graze on grass.

Tigers prefer to live in thick woods and rain forests.

Lions have huge, strong jaws. They have sharp teeth for cutting and tearing. The long canine teeth allow lions to hold on to an animal after they catch it.

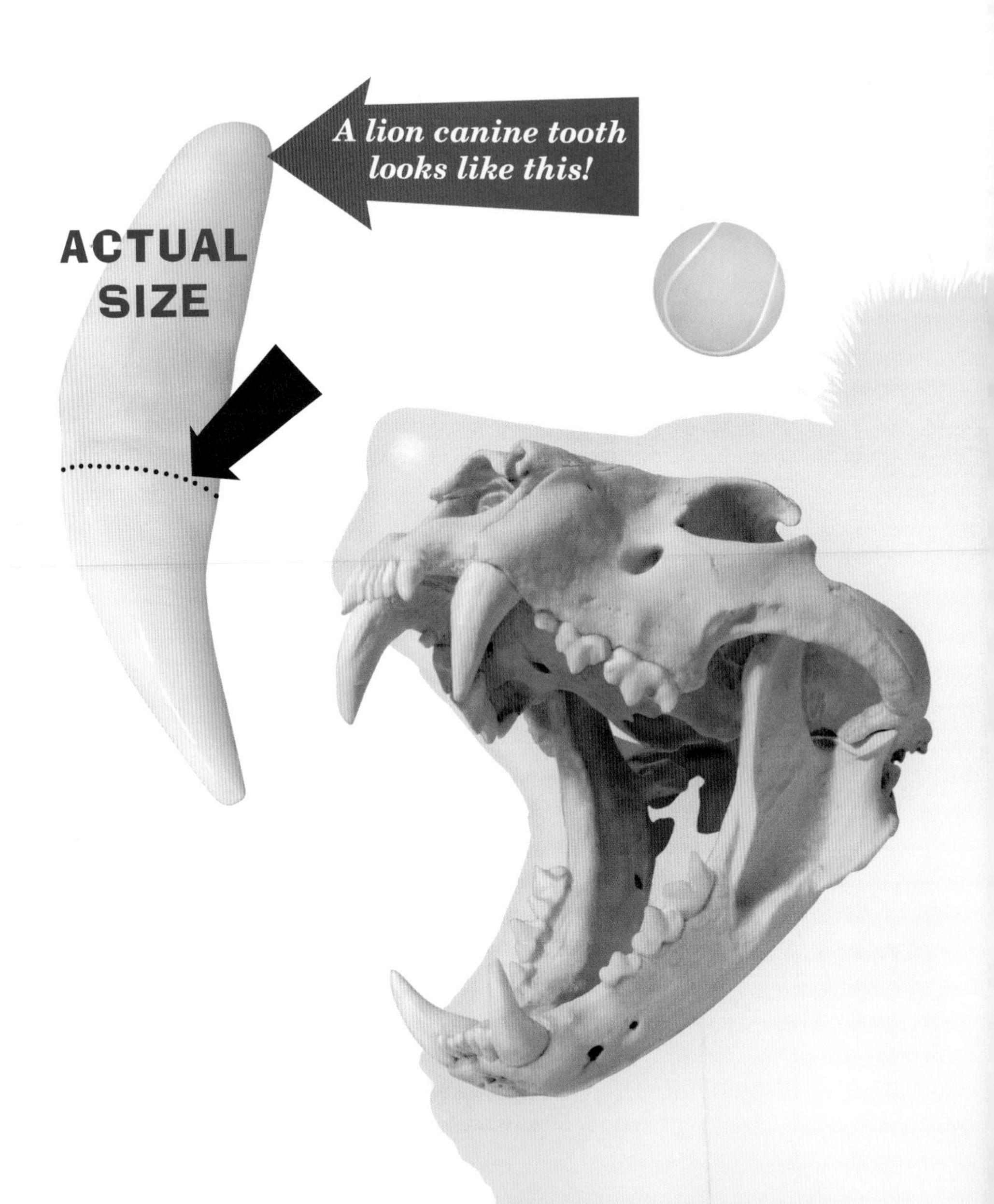

Lions have a big skull. But their brain is small, about the size of a tennis ball. Lions are not considered very smart.

Tigers also have a large skull, but their brain is only as big as a baseball. A small brain usually means that an animal is not smart. However, zookeepers have found tigers to be intelligent.

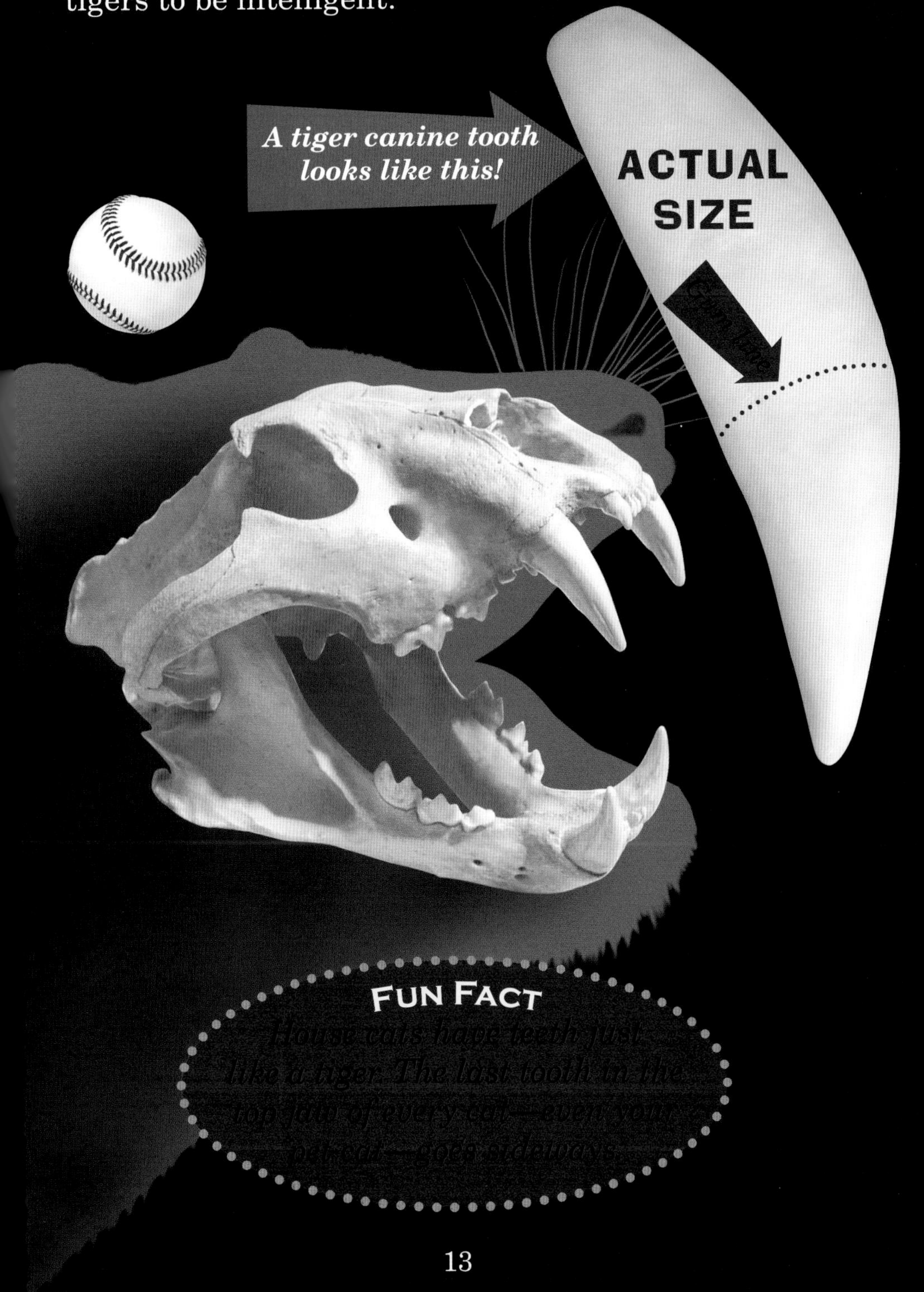

FUN FACT

House cats have teeth just like a tiger. The last tooth in the top jaw of every cat—even your pet cat—goes sideways.

Animals a lion eats

REMEMBER

"Eyes in front, like to hunt."
"Eyes on side, like to hide."

Lions are carnivores—they eat meat. They don't go to the supermarket or a restaurant. Lions are predators that hunt, catch, and eat other animals.

Tigers are also carnivores. They stalk, kill, and eat other animals. Tigers are clever and creative when hunting their prey.

Most of the time, lionesses do the hunting. They hunt in teams. The big male lions stay back and protect the cubs from attack.

DID YOU KNOW?

Don't think the male lion has an easy life. He is constantly fighting and being challenged by other big males for leadership.

Tigers usually hunt at night. Males and females each hunt alone. Tigers are sneakier than lions.

Interesting Fact

Hunters who go after tigers sometimes discover that the tiger is hunting *them*.

The male lion is the one with the big fuzzy mane around his neck. Female lions, or lionesses, have no manes.

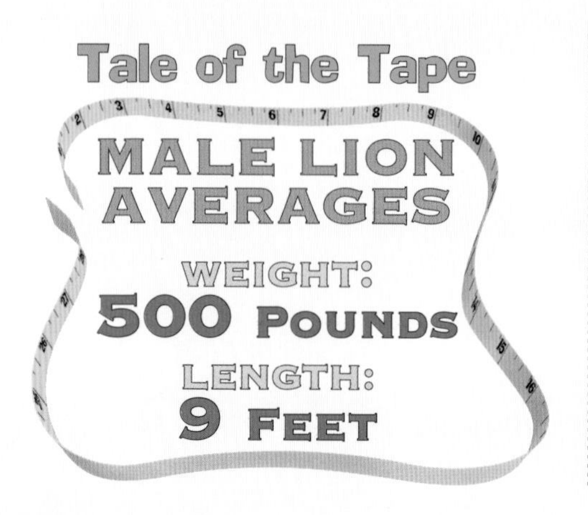

IMPORTANT FACT

The male lion's mane makes him look bigger and scarier and offers extra protection around his neck.

Lionesses average about two-thirds the size of male lions.

In a fight, who do you think would win? A lion or a tiger?

Male and female tigers look similar, but males are bigger. The males also have longer whiskers.

Female tigers average about two-thirds the size of male tigers.

Tale of the Tape

MALE TIGER AVERAGES

WEIGHT:
650 POUNDS

LENGTH:
10 FEET

So look at the facts! Who do you think has an advantage?

Lions have huge paws with long sharp claws. When walking, the claws do not touch the ground. But when provoked, the lion can extend its claws.

FUN FACT:
The claws are hidden by fur which is twice as long around the toes.

Lion's front left paw

Tigers also have huge paws. Tigers can leap fifteen feet high but can also quietly tiptoe like a ballerina. Lion and tiger footprints are called "pug marks."

DID YOU KNOW?

The back feet of lions and tigers have only four toes.

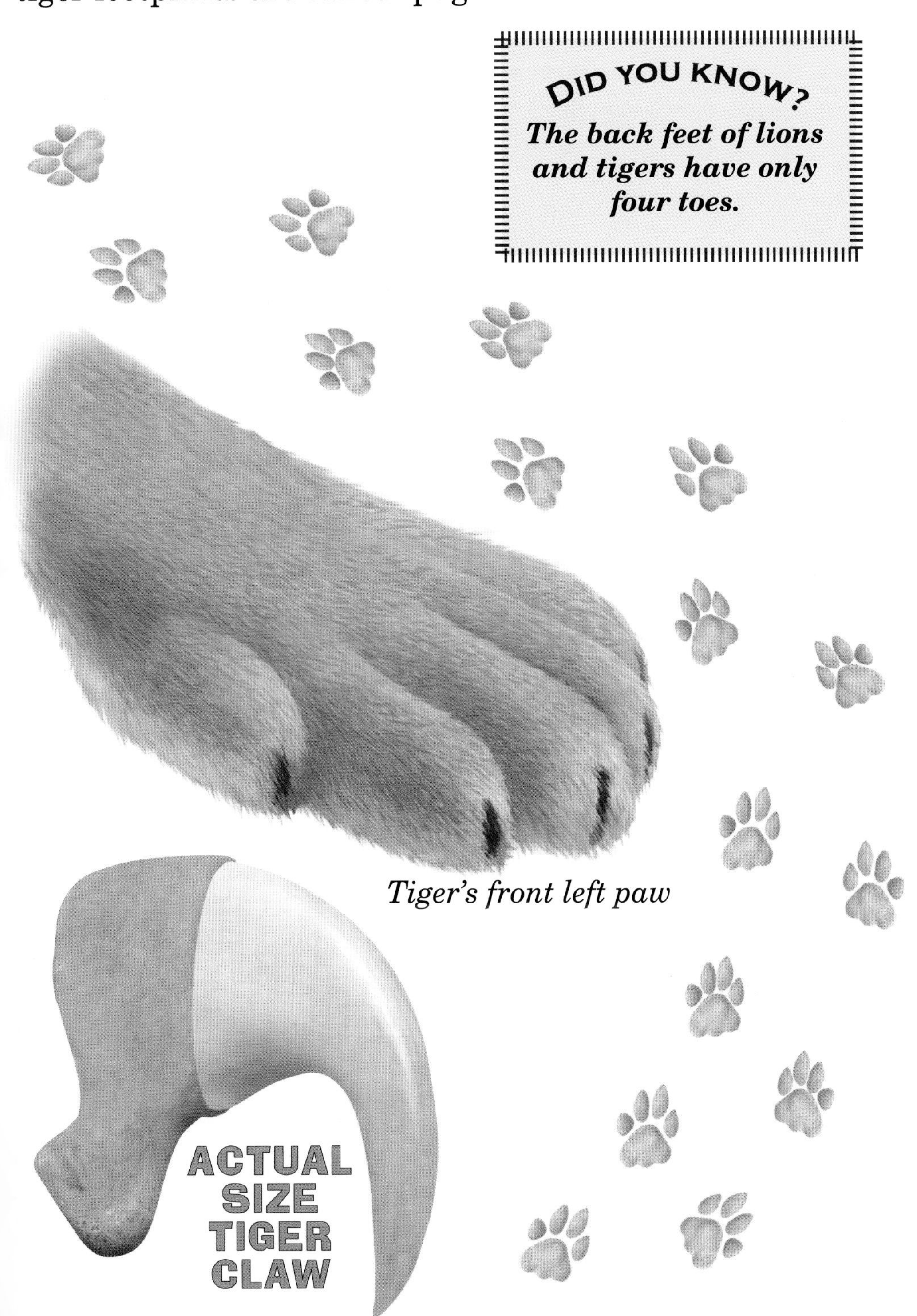

Tiger's front left paw

Lions live in family groups called prides. A typical pride includes three males, fifteen lionesses, and two dozen cubs. Lions are unique—they are the only wild cats who live in a family.

DID YOU KNOW?

A big male lion leads his pride for about two years. He is often challenged by other big males. The challenge usually ends in a fight to the death.

Tigers are shy and live alone. If they meet another tiger, they are usually friendly to each other.

Bonus Fact

Tigers might be found together when sharing a huge meal. A group of tigers is called a streak.

Baby lions are called cubs. Lion cubs are not plain brown. They are spotted. The spots help them to be camouflaged. As they grow up, they lose their spots.

DEFINITION

*The word **camouflaged** means able to hide or blend in with one's surroundings.*

DID YOU KNOW?

After a hunt, the male lion eats first, the lionesses eat next, and the cubs eat last.

Tiger cubs look like their parents. Tiger cubs are cute!

No, you cannot have one as a pet. When they grow up, they will eat you!

Lions have long tails and a clump of darker-colored fur on the end.

Tigers have long, striped tails.

Bonus Fact

A tiger's big tail helps it balance in a fight, or while climbing trees.

The lion has a Siberian tiger in his sights. He **roars**—lions are loud! They can be heard five miles away, frightening every creature around.

The tiger sees the lion and roars back. Tigers are not as loud as lions, but now every animal in the area is alert.

FUN FACT:
Tigers purr in between roars. Their purr sounds like "ooooooonnn" as they exhale!

The tiger waits as the lion makes the first move. They wrestle, teeth and claws bared. Both cats are up on their hind legs.

The tiger tries to bite the lion in the neck. It does no good. Every time the tiger bites the lion in the neck, it is like biting a giant hairball. The lion's mane gives the lion a defensive advantage.

The fight is vicious. The big cats bite and claw at each other. First the quick lion, then the agile tiger, is on top. The fight goes back and forth. Each cat is a magnificent fighter.

The tiger gets the advantage and bites the lion's neck again. However, the lion's mane is like biting a giant mattress. The tiger is a better fighter, but he is getting tired of biting a fur ball. Eventually the lion grabs the tiger by the neck.

The lion's bite causes fatal damage. The tiger is defeated.

The lion limps away in victory. It has many cuts and bruises.

The lion won today. Nature has given lions a wonderful gift—a big thick fuzzy mane.

Will a tiger ever be able to beat a lion?

RHINO

HIPPO

What would happen if a rhinoceros came face-to-face with a hippopotamus? What if they had a fight? Who do you think would win?

MEET A RHINO

Rhino is a shortened version of rhinoceros, which means "nose horn." They certainly do have horns. This is a white rhino.

FUN FACT
White rhinos cannot swim!

DID YOU KNOW?
The white rhino is the second-largest land mammal. Only elephants are bigger.

Scientific name: *Ceratotherium simum*.

MEET A HIPPO

Hippo is a shortened version of hippopotamus. Hippopotamus means "river horse." From now on, we will call them rhino and hippo.

FACT
Hippos are mammals.

DEFINITION
A mammal is a warm-blooded animal with fur or hair that gives milk to its young.

Scientific name: *Hippopotamus amphibius*

TYPES OF RHINOS

There are five species of rhinos.

WHITE RHINO

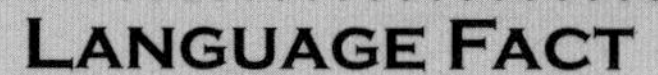

LANGUAGE FACT

White rhino's name may have come from the Dutch word weid. *It means "wide," as in wide lips.*

COLOR FACT

White rhinos and black rhinos actually are both gray and look alike.

INDIAN RHINO

BLACK RHINO

HORN FACT

Indian and Javan rhinos have only one horn.

JAVAN RHINO

SUMATRAN RHINO

TYPES OF HIPPOS

There are two species of hippos.

HIPPOPOTAMUS

HEIGHT FACT
The pygmy hippo is half as tall as a hippopotamus.

PYGMY HIPPO

DID YOU KNOW?
The pygmy hippo weighs only one-fourth as much as a hippo.

WHITE RHINO TERRITORY

White rhinos live in Africa.

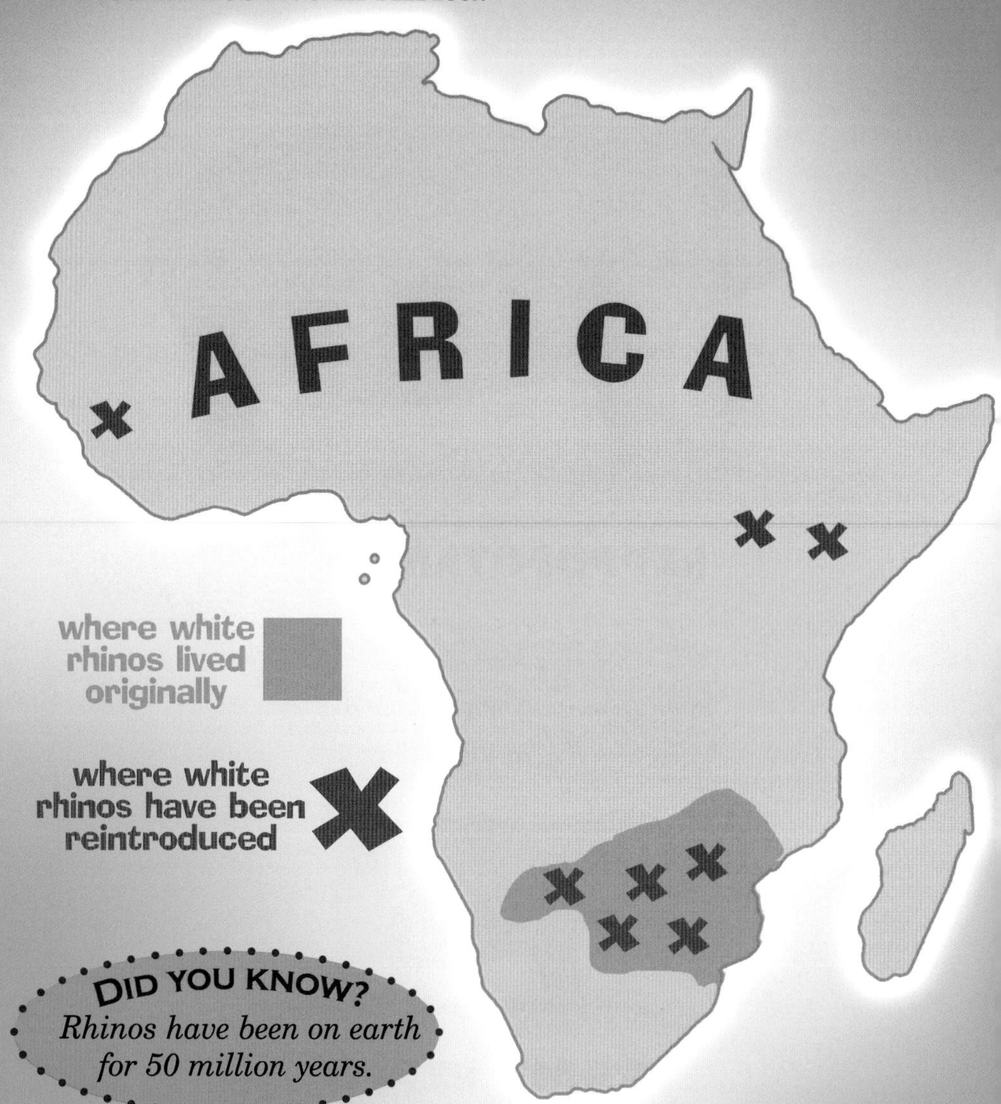

DID YOU KNOW?
Rhinos have been on earth for 50 million years.

FUN FACT
Rhinos live in grasslands and savannas.

DEFINITION
A savanna is a grassy area with few trees.

HIPPO TERRITORY

Hippos also live in Africa.

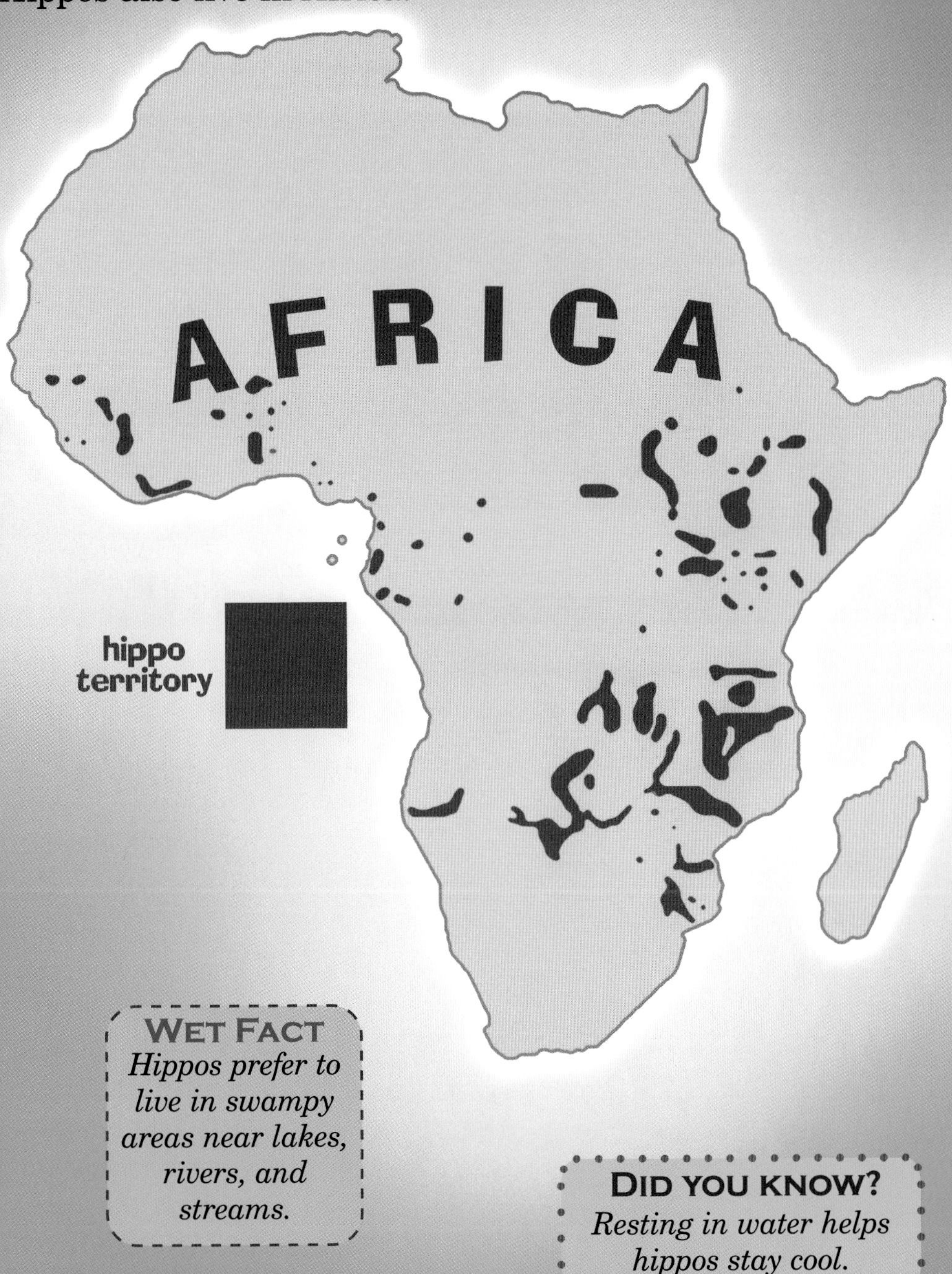

WET FACT
Hippos prefer to live in swampy areas near lakes, rivers, and streams.

DID YOU KNOW?
Resting in water helps hippos stay cool.

RHINO DIET

White rhinos eat grass. Grass, grass, and more grass. Rhinos are not meat eaters; they have no interest in eating a hippo. White rhinos have wide lips. They pull up grass with their lips. They chew the grass with their back molars

DEFINITION
Grass eaters are called grazers.

RHINO BABY

This is a baby rhino.

TUMMY FACT
A rhino has four sections to its stomach. It takes a lot to digest grass.

FUN FACT
When rhinos are born, they can weigh up to 90 pounds.

HIPPO DIET

Hippos also eat grass and some leaves. They prefer to eat at night. They rest during the day.

FACT
Areas that have been eaten by hippos are called "hippo lawns."

HIPPO BABY

DID YOU KNOW?
A baby hippo weighs between 60–100 pounds.

RHINOCEROS SKELETON

A rhinoceros is a vertebrate animal. Vertebrates have backbones just like humans.

DID YOU KNOW?
A rhinoceros has a heavy head.

FACT
The Xyloryctes jamaicensis *is a rhinoceros beetle.*

This insect shares its name with the rhino.

HIPPOPOTAMUS SKELETON

A hippo is also a vertebrate. Its spinal cord runs from its brain to its tail.

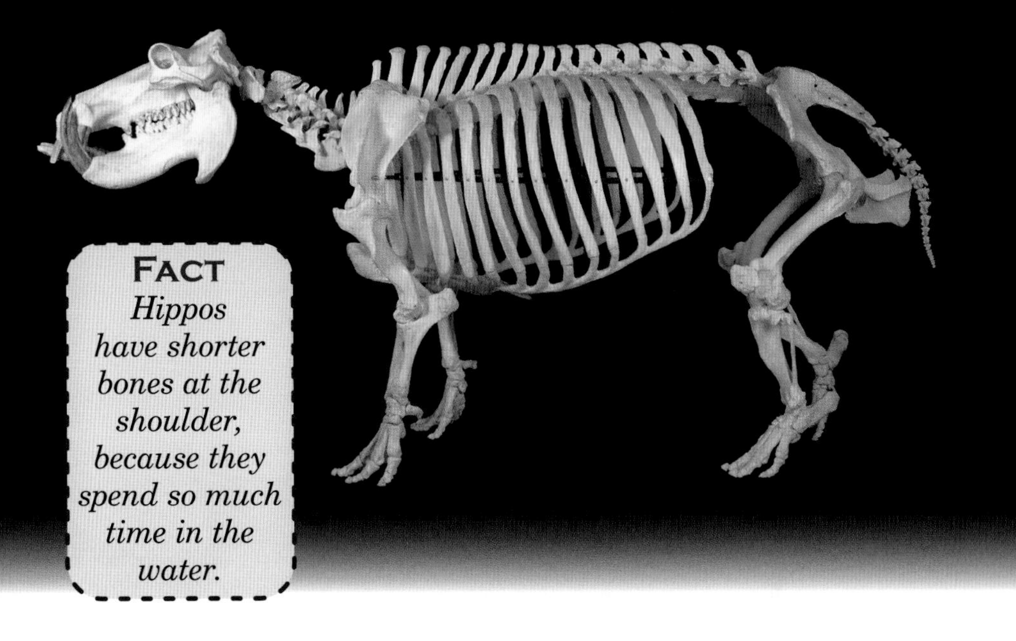

FACT
Hippos have shorter bones at the shoulder, because they spend so much time in the water.

This is a hippopotamus beetle.

FACT?
The hippo beetle's scientific name is Royis wandelirius.

DID YOU KNOW?
One of the insects on these two pages is fake. Which one?

FREE RIDE

How would you like to ride around on a rhino? That is what oxpeckers do. These birds eat ticks, fleas, blood-sucking flies, and insect larvae off the backs of rhinos.

GROSS FACT
Oxpeckers also eat earwax.

FUN FACT
Oxpeckers are also called tickbirds.

COLOR FACT
Oxpeckers are easy to recognize; they have red eyes and red beaks.

Oxpeckers live only where there are larger mammals. They also like to ride on cattle, giraffes, zebra, and buffalo. Some scientists think it is a mutual relationship in which rhino and oxpecker both benefit. Others think the bird is a parasite.

FREE CLEANING

The hippo loves the water. One reason might be the carp that clean its teeth, hide, and lips.

LOVELY FACT
There is also a fish that follows hippos and eats their waste.

DEFINITION
A carp is a type of freshwater fish.

FACT
A hippo can hold its breath for five minutes.

Hippos love freshwater, and so do humans. This sometimes creates conflicts between people and hippos.

RHINO FOOT

A rhino foot has three toes.

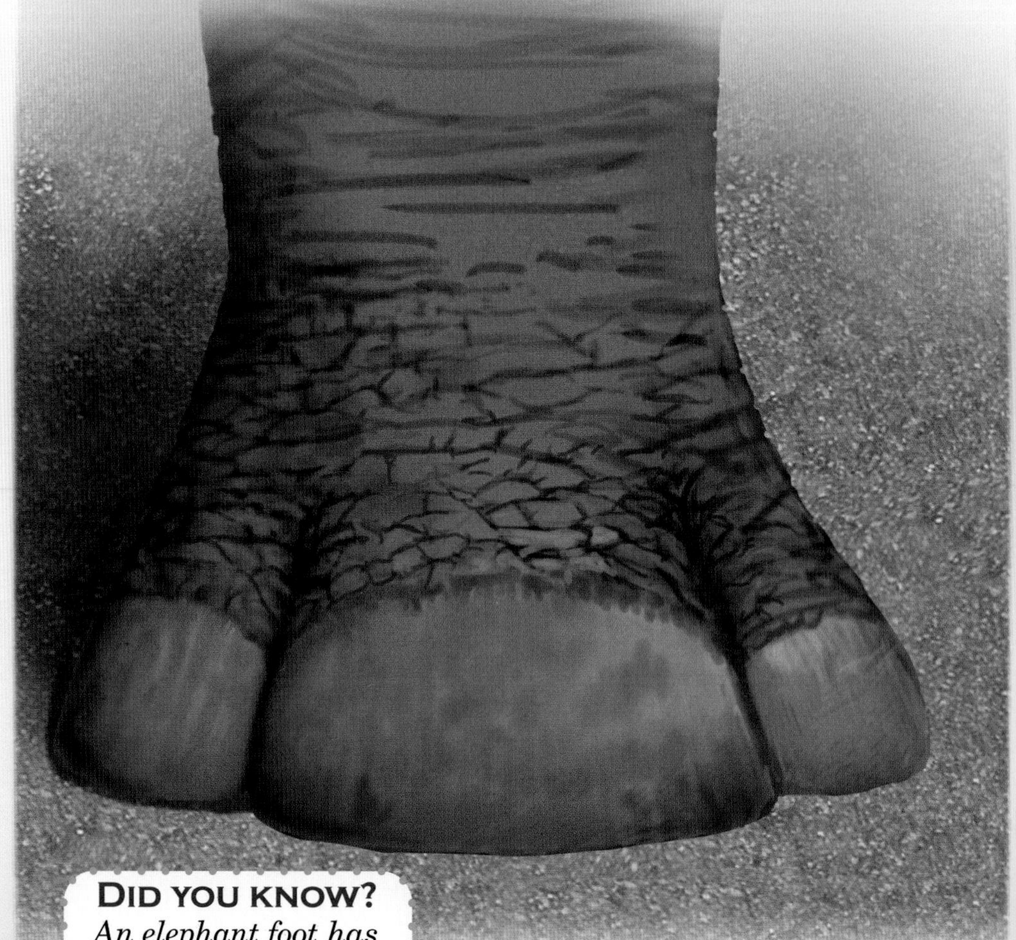

DID YOU KNOW?
An elephant foot has five toes.

Largest land mammal

Second-largest land mammal

HIPPO TOES

A hippo foot has four toes.

MATH FACT
Four is an even number. Some animals have an even number of toes, and some have an odd number of toes.

FACT
A horse foot has one toe.

Third-largest land mammal

hippo

Largest mammal: blue whale

human

RHINO WEAPONS

A rhino's best weapon is its size. It is huge! Rhinos stand six feet high at the shoulders and weigh 8,000 pounds.

FUN FACT

The rhino's horn is made of keratin. Keratin is the same material your hair and fingernails are made of.

4 TONS

DID YOU KNOW?

8,000 pounds equals 4 tons.

HIPPO WEAPONS

The hippo's best weapons are its huge teeth and strong jaw. It has six big front teeth on its upper jaw and four teeth plus two long tusks on its lower jaw. It chews with its back molars.

FACT

Elephants, hippos, walrus, and wild boars have tusks.

DEFINITION

A tusk is a long, pointed tooth. Tusks are usually found in pairs.

3 TONS

A hippo's size is also a great weapon!

RHINO SKIN

Rhinos are mammals but they have almost no hair.

FACT
Rhinos roll in the mud to protect their skin from the hot sun.

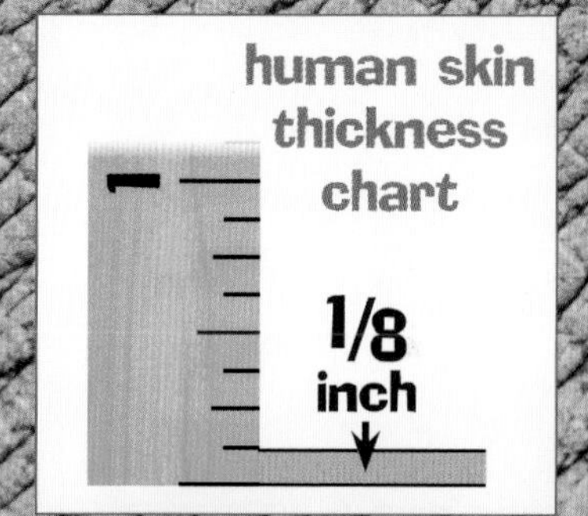

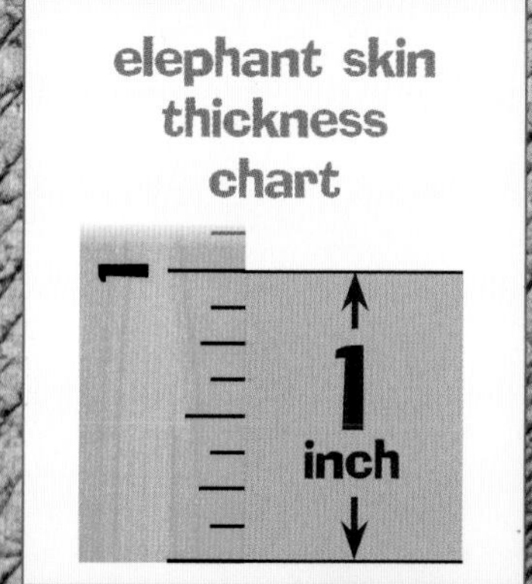

HIPPO SKIN

Hippos also have almost no hair.

FANTASTIC FACT!
Hippo skin looks like armor, but it is actually very sensitive.

IT'S NOT BLOOD!
Hippos have a natural skin lotion. Their skin oozes a reddish-orange oil.

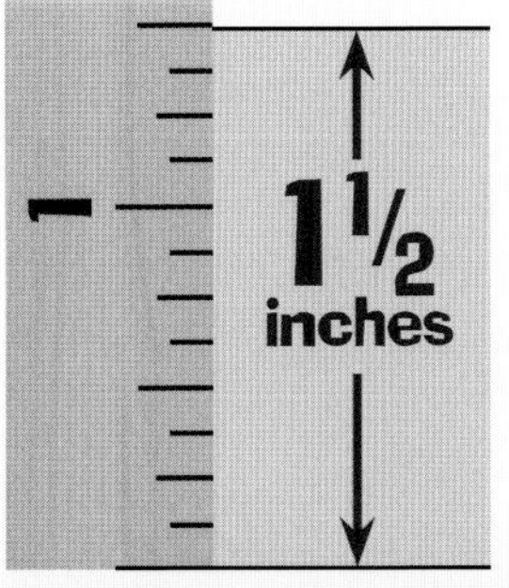

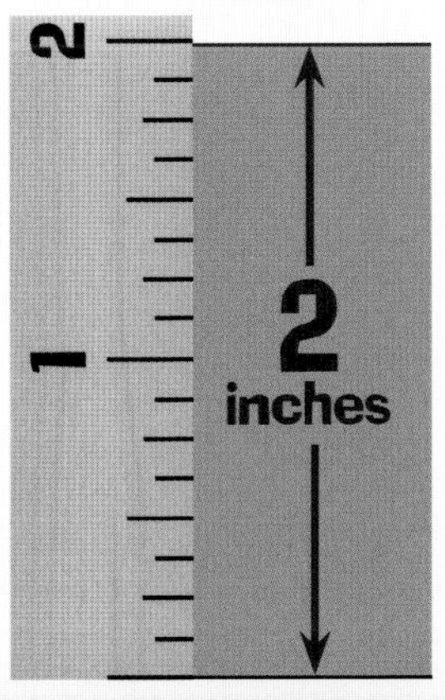

I HEAR YOU

The rhino can swivel its ears in different directions. It has excellent hearing.

DEFINITION
A group of rhinos is called a crash.

DID YOU KNOW?
A rhino can smell and hear a lion before it sees it.

I SEE YOU

The hippo's head is beautifully designed. When swimming, its ears, nose, and eyes are above water. It is always on the lookout.

DEFINITION
A group of hippos is called a bloat.

DID YOU KNOW?
A hippo can sleep underwater. While sleeping, it surfaces every five minutes to breathe.

RHINO SPEED

In short bursts, a rhino can run 30 miles per hour.

RUNNING FACT
A rhino can easily outrun a human.

FUN FACT
A rhinoceros can gallop like a horse.

HIPPO SPEED

A hippo can run about 18 miles per hour. A hippo has no interest in running a marathon. It's not designed for long-distance running.

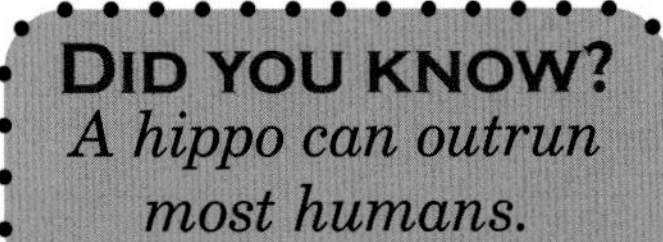

DID YOU KNOW?
A hippo can outrun most humans.

DID YOU KNOW?
According to zoologists, the closest known relatives to hippos are dolphins and whales.

DEFINITION
A zoologist is a scientist who studies animals and animal behavior.

LISTEN!

I told the illustrator not to show the rhino's rear end, but he did!

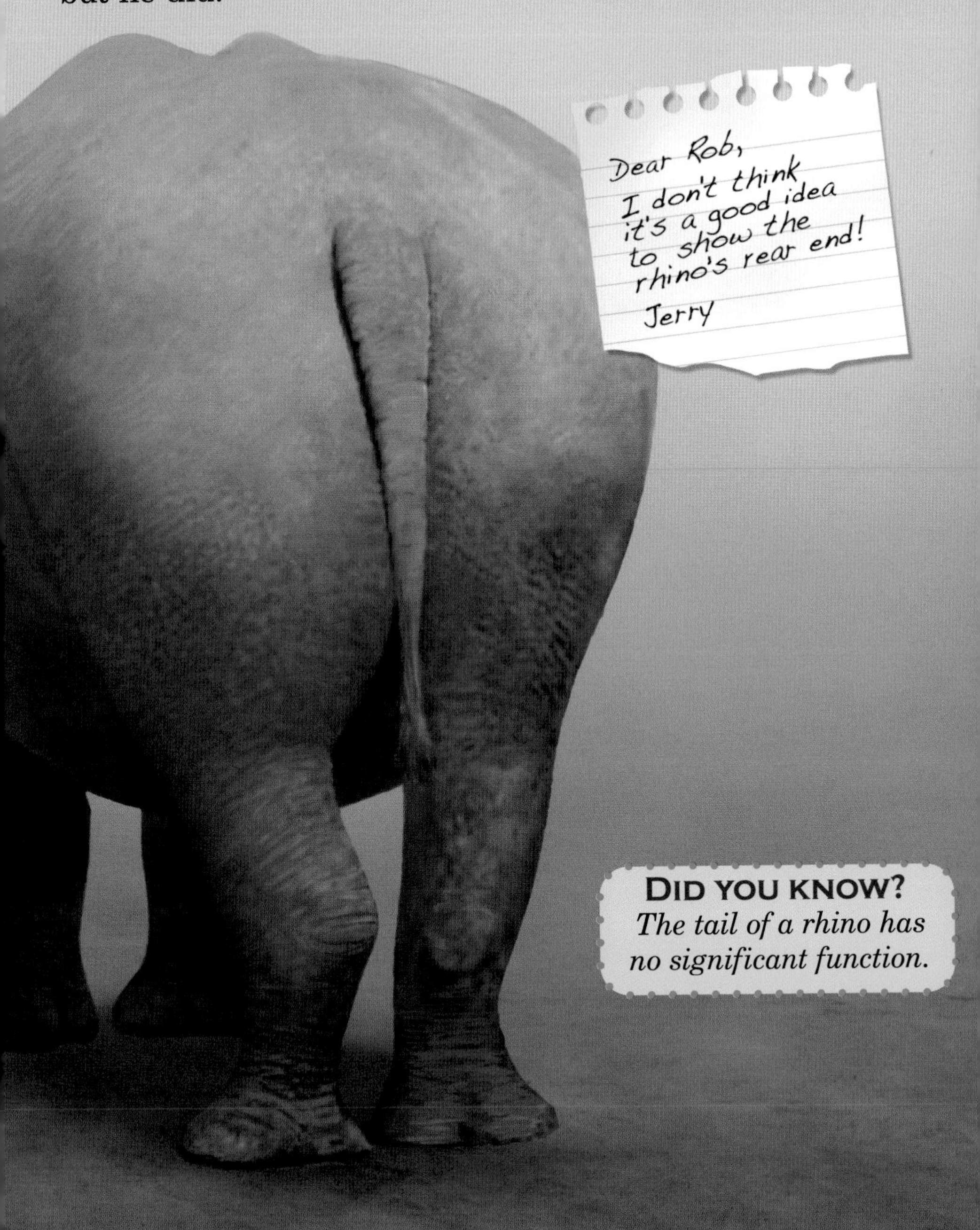

DID YOU KNOW?
The tail of a rhino has no significant function.

DON'T DO IT!

I asked the illustrator not to show the hippo's rear end, either!

DID YOU KNOW?
From behind, the hippo and the rhino look similar.

The hippo has a small tail. It's not long like a snow leopard tail, not fluffy like a horse tail, and not good for balance like a kangaroo tail.

The thirsty rhino walks over to the watering hole.

As the rhino takes a drink, the hippo opens its mouth and scares the rhino away. The thirsty rhino tries again. The hippo opens its big mouth, and the frightened rhino backs off.

Later, the hippo wants a drink. This time, the rhino charges and chases the hippo. The hippo returns. The rhino lowers its head and flashes its horns, and the hippo runs away.

Rhinos don't eat hippos. Hippos don't eat rhinos. But they are fighting for the same water.

Again the hippo opens its mouth, and the rhino runs away.

The rhino returns and charges the hippo. At the last second, the hippo turns around and opens its powerful jaws. The rhino retreats.

The rhino slowly walks back, with its head down and horns ready. The hippo swings around quickly and bites the rhino on its hind leg. Ouch! The rhino's leg is broken. It limps away.

The rhino has made a fatal mistake.

WHO WOULD WIN?®

WALRUS

VS.

ELEPHANT SEAL

What would happen if a walrus swam into an elephant seal? What if they had a fight? If they met on land, on ice, or in the ocean, who do you think would win?

Fin Fact

Seals are in a group of animals called pinnipeds. Pinniped means "finned feet."

MEET A WALRUS

There are two types of walruses: Atlantic walruses and Pacific walruses. Atlantic walruses range from Canada to Greenland. Scientific name: *Odobenus rosmarus rosmaru*

The Arctic is the northernmost area of the Earth. Polar bears live in the Arctic, but not penguins. The Arctic also has walruses.

MEET AN ELEPHANT SEAL

There are two kinds of elephant seals: northern elephant seals and southern elephant seals.
Scientific name: *Mirounga angustirostris*

BIG AND BIGGER
Male northern elephant seals are three times heavier than females.

northern elephant seal

Northern elephant seals live in the northern hemisphere, mostly along the western coast of the US, Mexico, and Canada.

NORTHERN HEMISPHERE

northern elephant seal territory

VIEW OF EARTH FROM ABOVE THE NORTH POLE

Africa
Europe
Asia
ARCTIC CIRCLE
ATLANTIC OCEAN
North Pole
ARCTIC OCEAN
South America
North America
PACIFIC OCEAN

MEET ANOTHER WALRUS

Pacific walruses live on the coasts of Russia and Alaska.
Scientific name: *Odobenus rosmarus*
Its scientific name means "tooth-walking seahorse."

FACT
A walrus is a seal.

MEET ANOTHER ELEPHANT SEAL

Southern elephant seals live in the sub-Antarctic and Antarctic. Scientific name: *Mirounga leonina*

DID YOU KNOW?
The Antarctic region has penguins, but no polar bears or walruses.

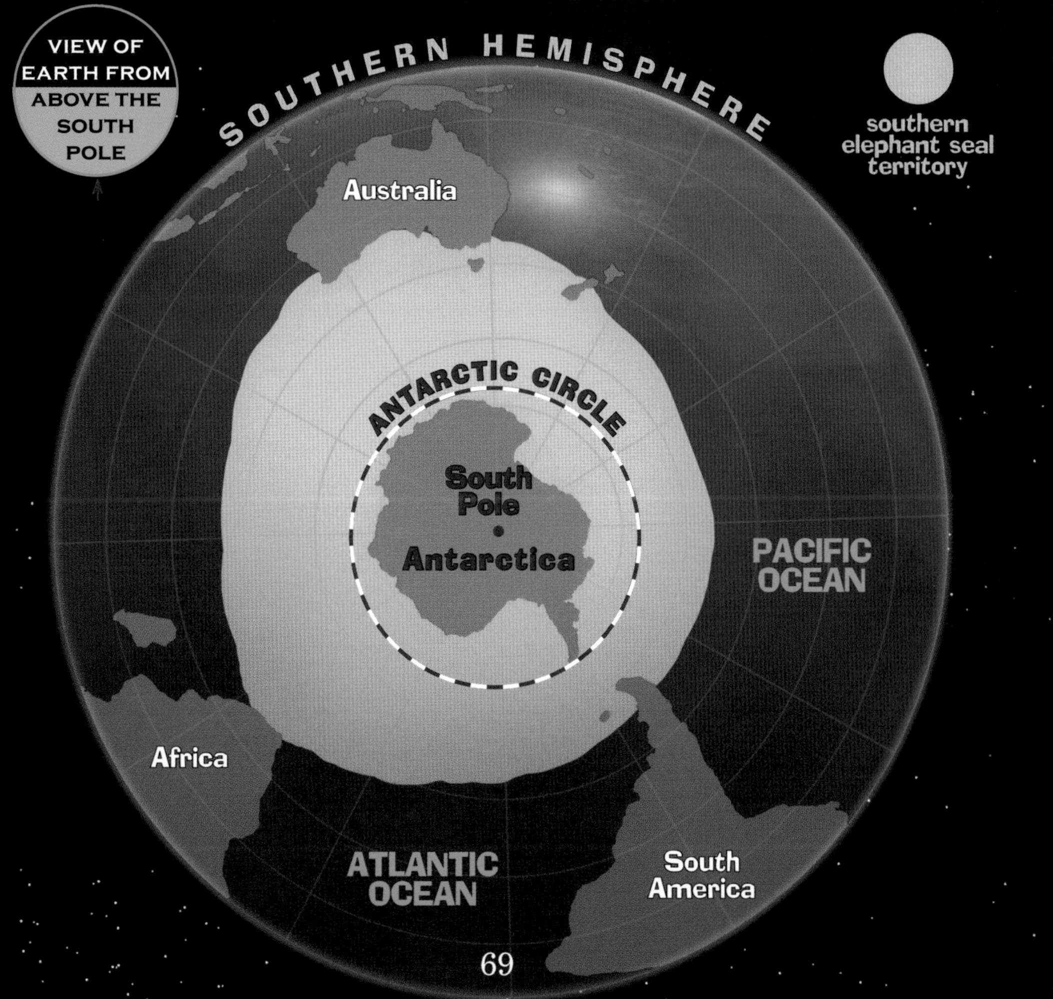

southern elephant seal

Let's see, walruses live in the northern hemisphere, and southern elephant seals live in the southern hemisphere. They wouldn't meet in real life. But we'll let them meet in this book. The walrus in this book will be the Pacific walrus.

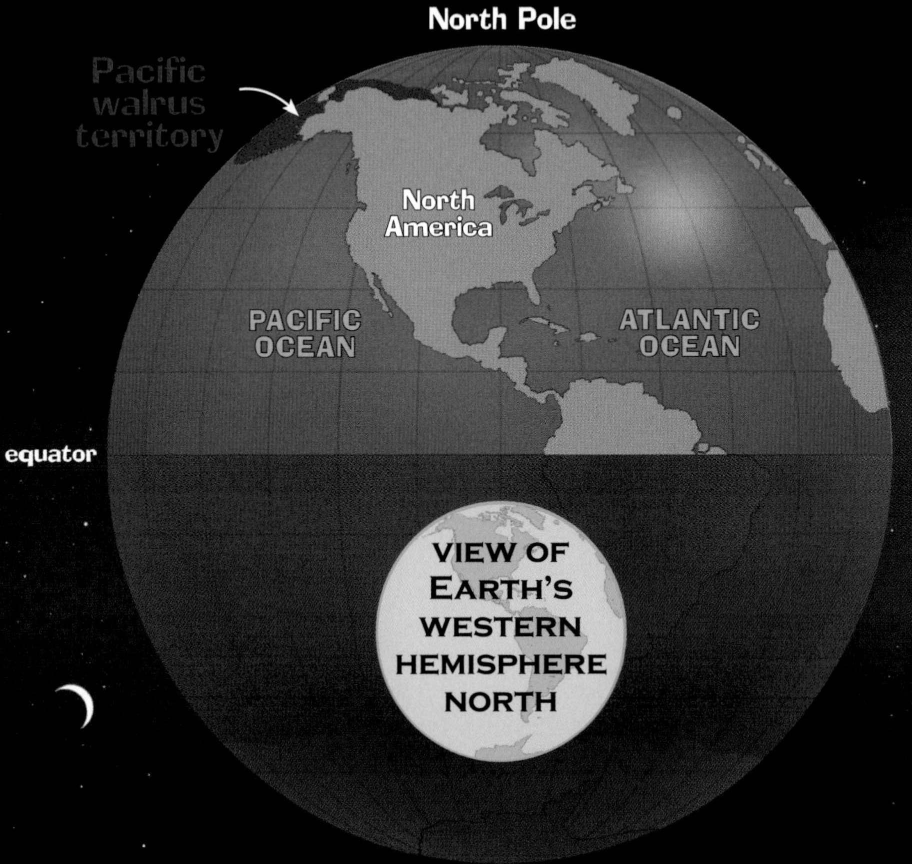

Weight and Size

Male Pacific walruses can weigh up to 4,000 lbs. They can grow up to 12 feet long.

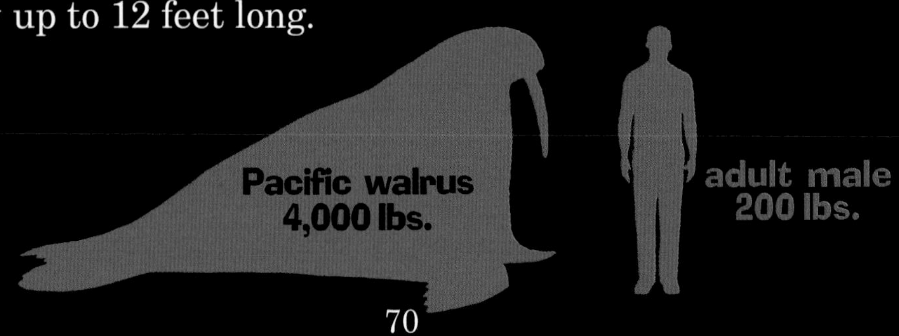

DECIDE

From now on the elephant seal in this book will be the southern elephant seal.

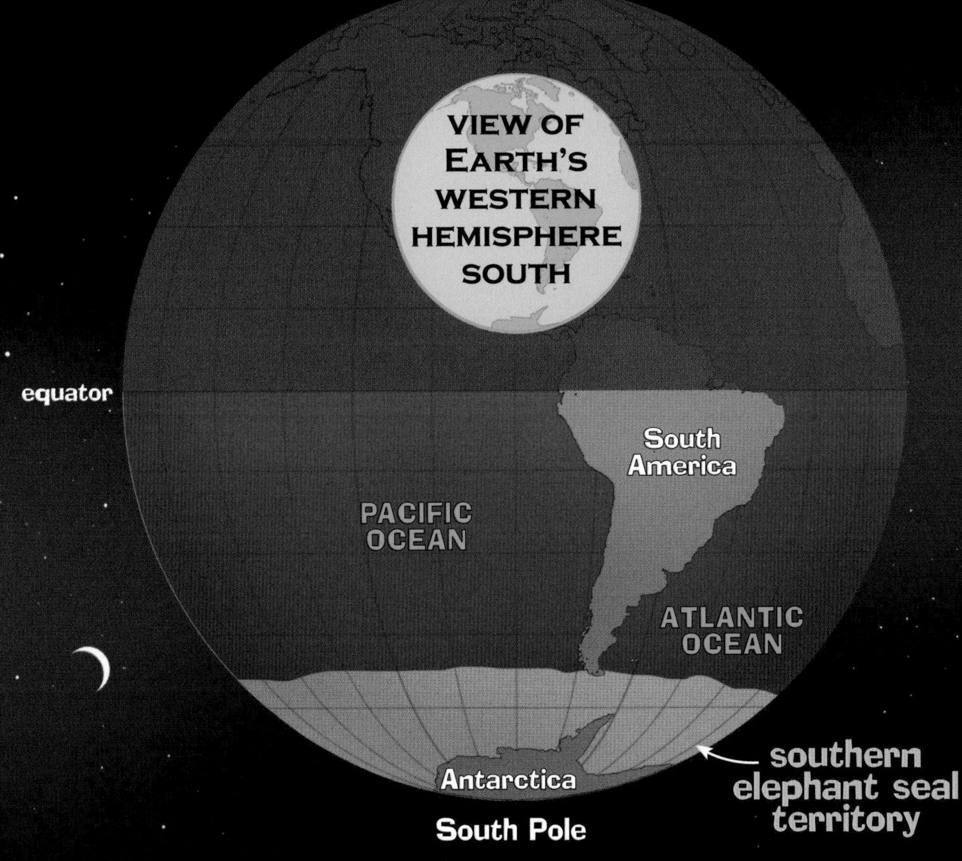

Weight and Size

Male southern elephant seals can weigh up to 8,800 lbs. They can grow more than 20 feet long. The southern elephant seal is the largest carnivorous mammal that is not a whale.

DEFINITION
A carnivore is an animal that eats meat.

first-grade girl 52 lbs.

southern elephant seal 8,800 lbs.

TUSKS

What is most noticeable about walruses? Their tusks! Walrus tusks can be more than 3 feet long. Tusks help walruses defend themselves from killer whales or polar bears.

Another noticeable thing about walruses? Their long whiskers.

WHISKER FACT
Walruses' whiskers are called vibrissae. The whiskers pick up vibrations in the water and on the ocean floor.

Walruses, like other earless seals, have earholes in the side of their heads but no earflaps.

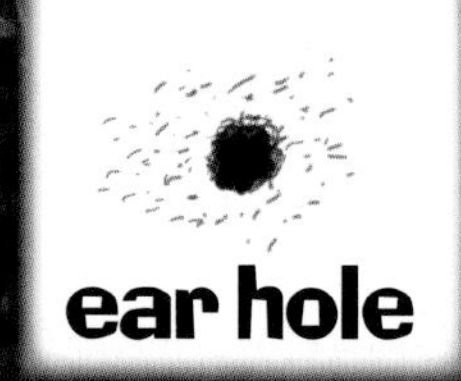

EAR FACT
There are two types of seals: earless seals and eared seals.

SNOUT

What is most noticeable about male elephant seals? Their snouts. They are used mostly for making noise.

SNOUT FACT
Female elephant seals do not have an enlarged snout.

Elephant seals are also earless seals. They have no earflaps.

MORE TUSKS

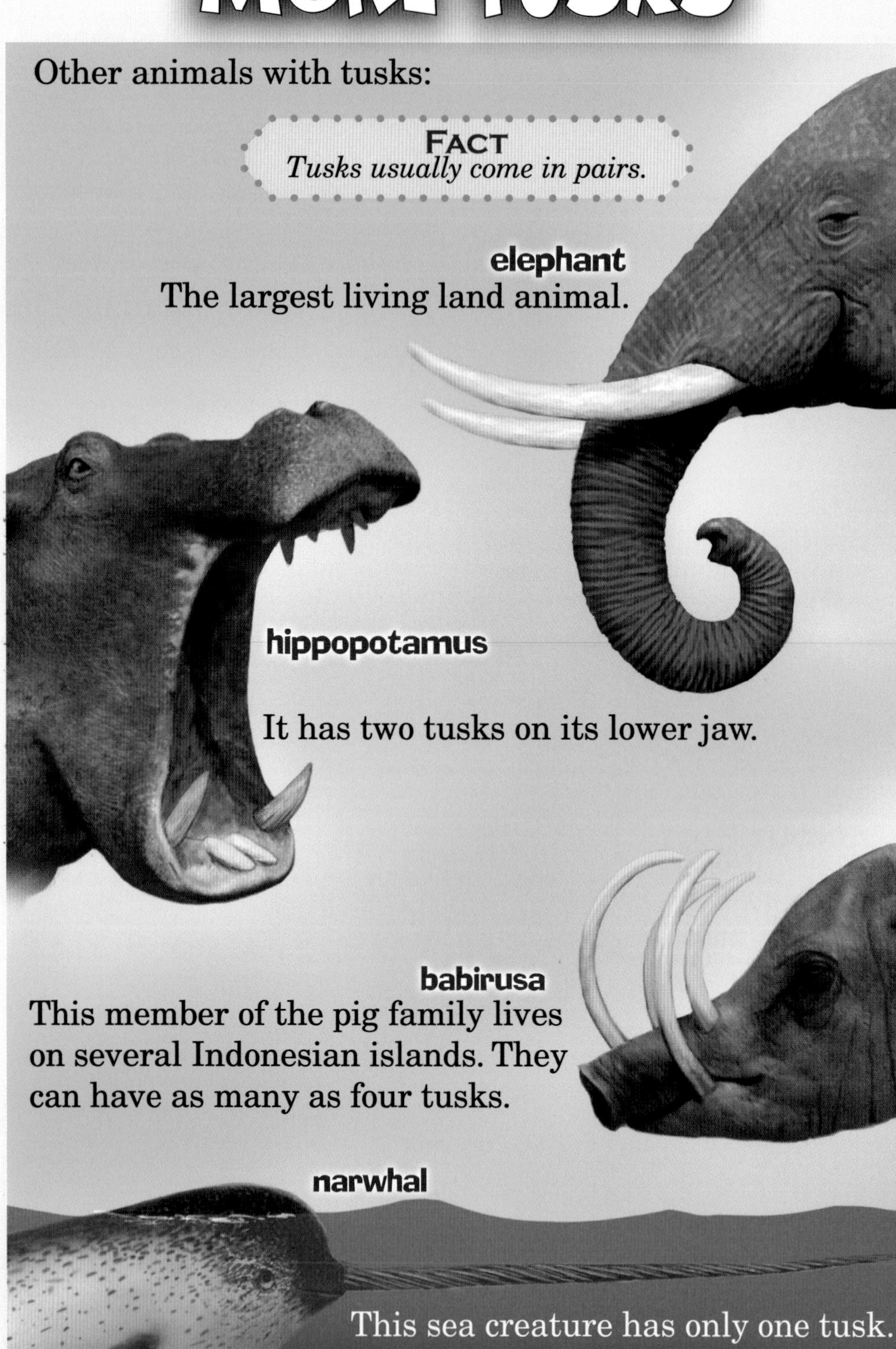

Other animals with tusks:

FACT
Tusks usually come in pairs.

elephant
The largest living land animal.

hippopotamus
It has two tusks on its lower jaw.

babirusa
This member of the pig family lives on several Indonesian islands. They can have as many as four tusks.

narwhal
This sea creature has only one tusk.

OTHER SNOUTS

Other animals with enlarged snouts:

BONUS FACT
An elephant has 40,000 muscles in its trunk.

FAT

Walrus skin is up to 1.5 inches thick. Walrus blubber, or fat, is up to 4 inches thick. Blubber keeps walruses warm. Walruses can comfortably swim in freezing-cold water or sit on ice without getting cold.

DEFINITION
Blubber is the fat in sea mammals.

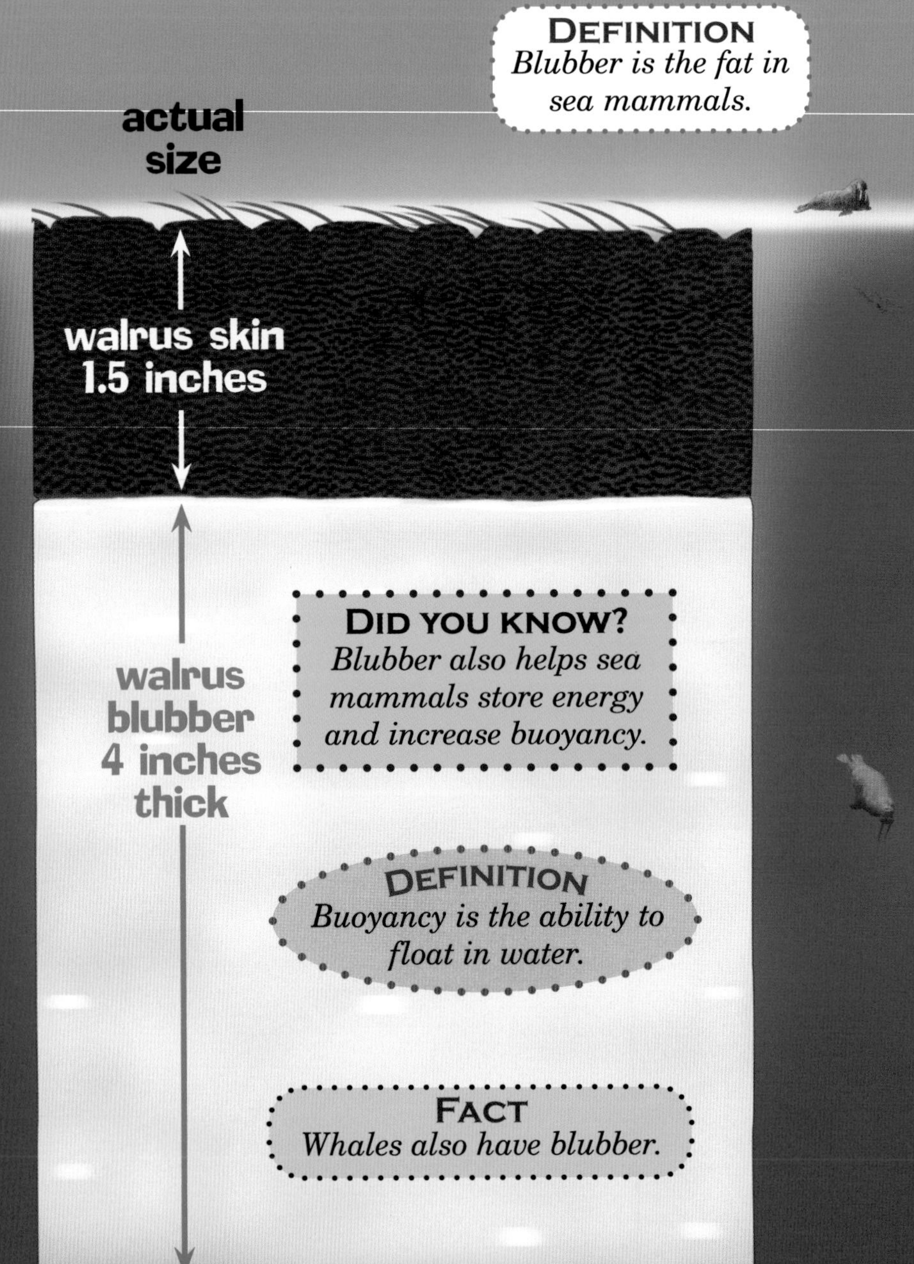

DID YOU KNOW?
Blubber also helps sea mammals store energy and increase buoyancy.

DEFINITION
Buoyancy is the ability to float in water.

FACT
Whales also have blubber.

BLUBBER

Elephant seals also have thick skin and a layer of blubber. While many mammals grow new hair and skin over time, an elephant seal replaces their skin and fur all at once. Every year elephant seals molt, or replace, their fur.

CONSERVATION FACT
Sea mammals are protected by the Marine Mammal Protection Act.

DID YOU KNOW?
Elephant seal blubber was often used to make lamp oil.

WALRUS PARTS

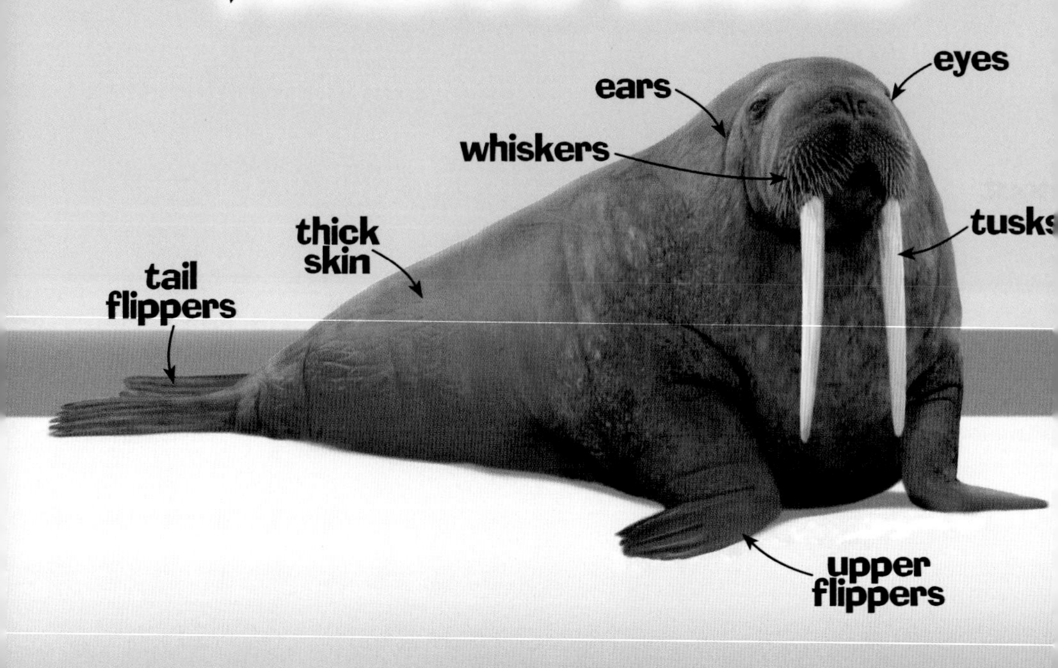

BABY FACT
A baby walrus is called a pup or calf.

baby walrus

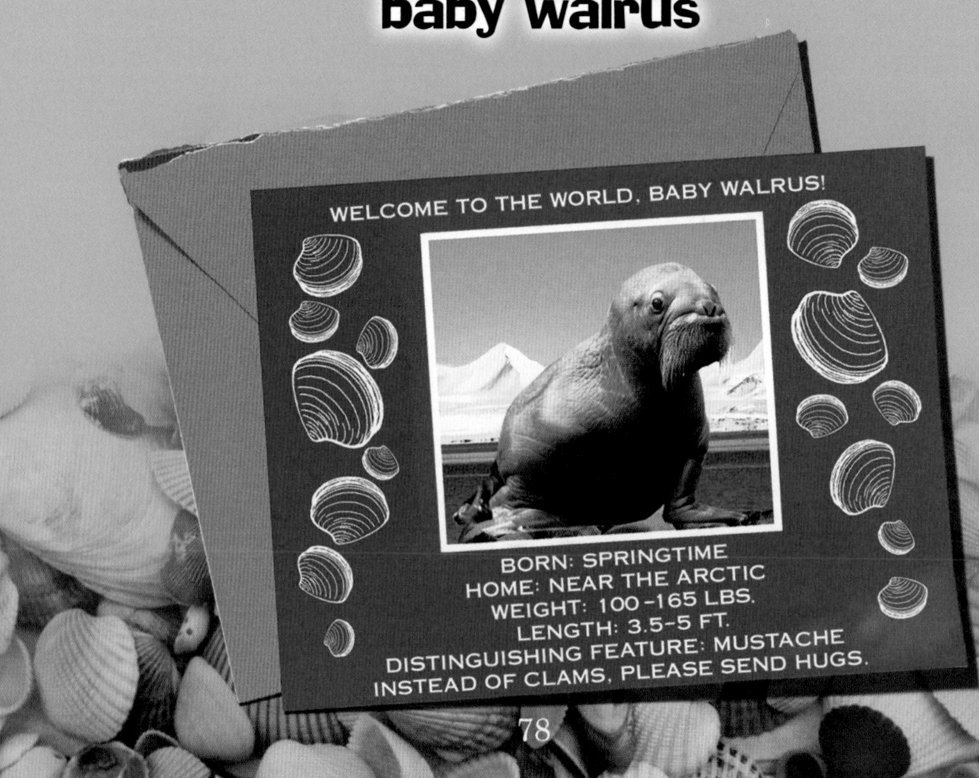

ELEPHANT SEAL PARTS

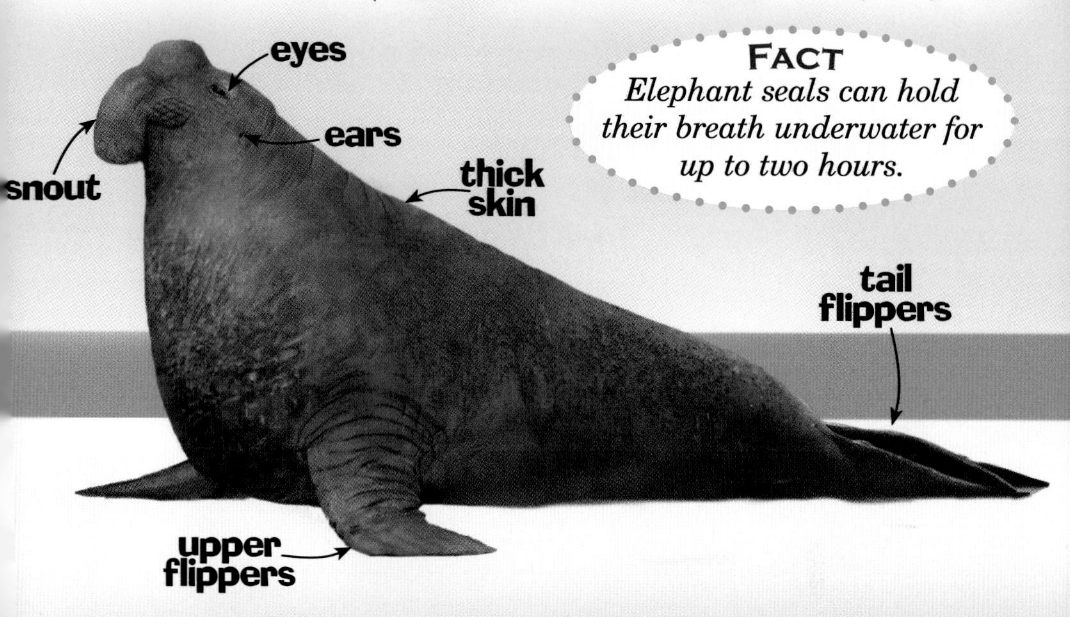

FACT
Elephant seals can hold their breath underwater for up to two hours.

BABY FACT
A baby elephant seal is called a pup.

baby elephant seal

FLIPPERS

Walruses do not have arms and legs; they have flippers. They propel themselves in the water with their tail flippers. They steer with their upper flippers.

FLIPPER FACT
Fur seals steer with their tails and swim with their upper flippers.

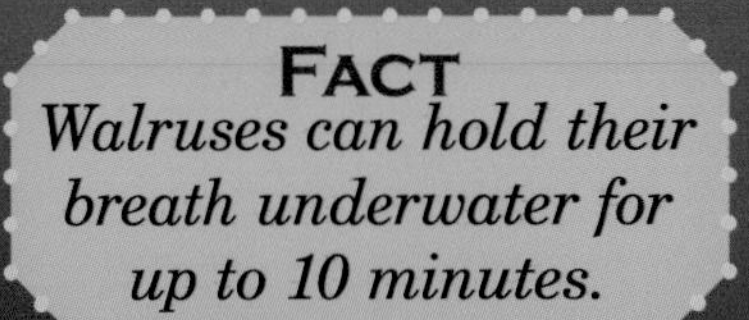

FACT
Walruses can hold their breath underwater for up to 10 minutes.

SPEED

On land, walruses crawl slowly, only about 5 mph. They're much faster in the water, swimming up to 22 mph.

WEBBING

Flippers of elephant seals have five digits. Their “fingers” are webbed.

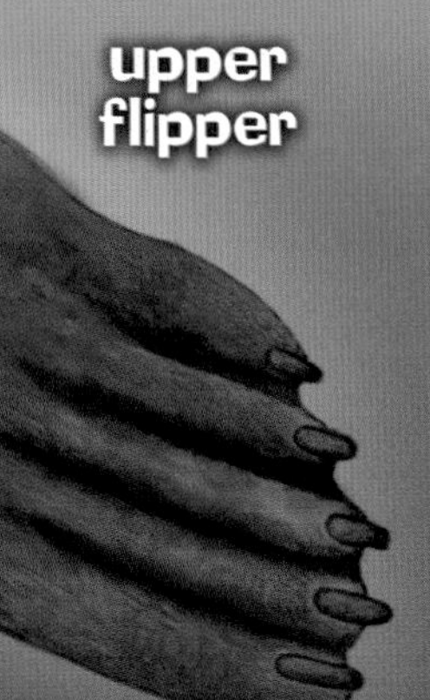

FLIPPER FACT

Like walruses, elephant seals also propel themselves with their tail flippers and steer with upper flippers.

SPEED

Elephant seals are also slow on land, flopping at about 5 mph. But they swim quickly, reaching speeds of 10–15 mph. The fastest human swimmers reach only about 5–6 mph.

crawling

swimming

AWESOME SEAL FACTS

WET FACT
Most seals live in the ocean. However, there is one species of seal that lives exclusively in freshwater. It lives in Lake Baikal, Russia. It is called a nerpa or a Baikal seal.

Smallest Seal

The nerpa is the smallest seal in the world.

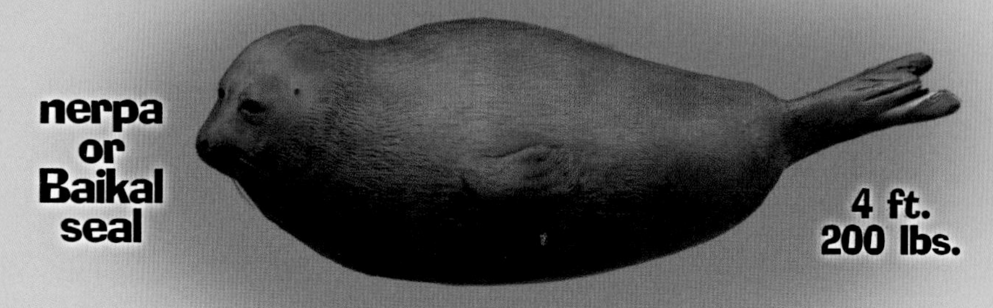

Smallest Ocean Seal

The smallest ocean seal is the ringed seal.

DIVE FACT
Walruses dive down to 250 feet. They prefer shallow water, where they can find shellfish.

MORE ABOUT SEALS

tanker

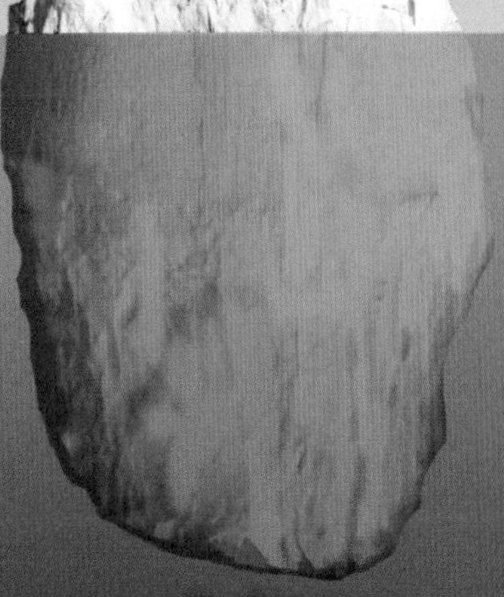

iceberg

DIVE FACT
Elephant seals can dive down to 1 mile deep searching for food.

HISTORY FACT
Elephant seals were almost hunted to extinction for the oil in their blubber.

oil lamp

DEFINITION
Extinction is when a species dies out completely.

1 mile

COMPARE

Here is a walrus skull. Walruses eat mostly clams.

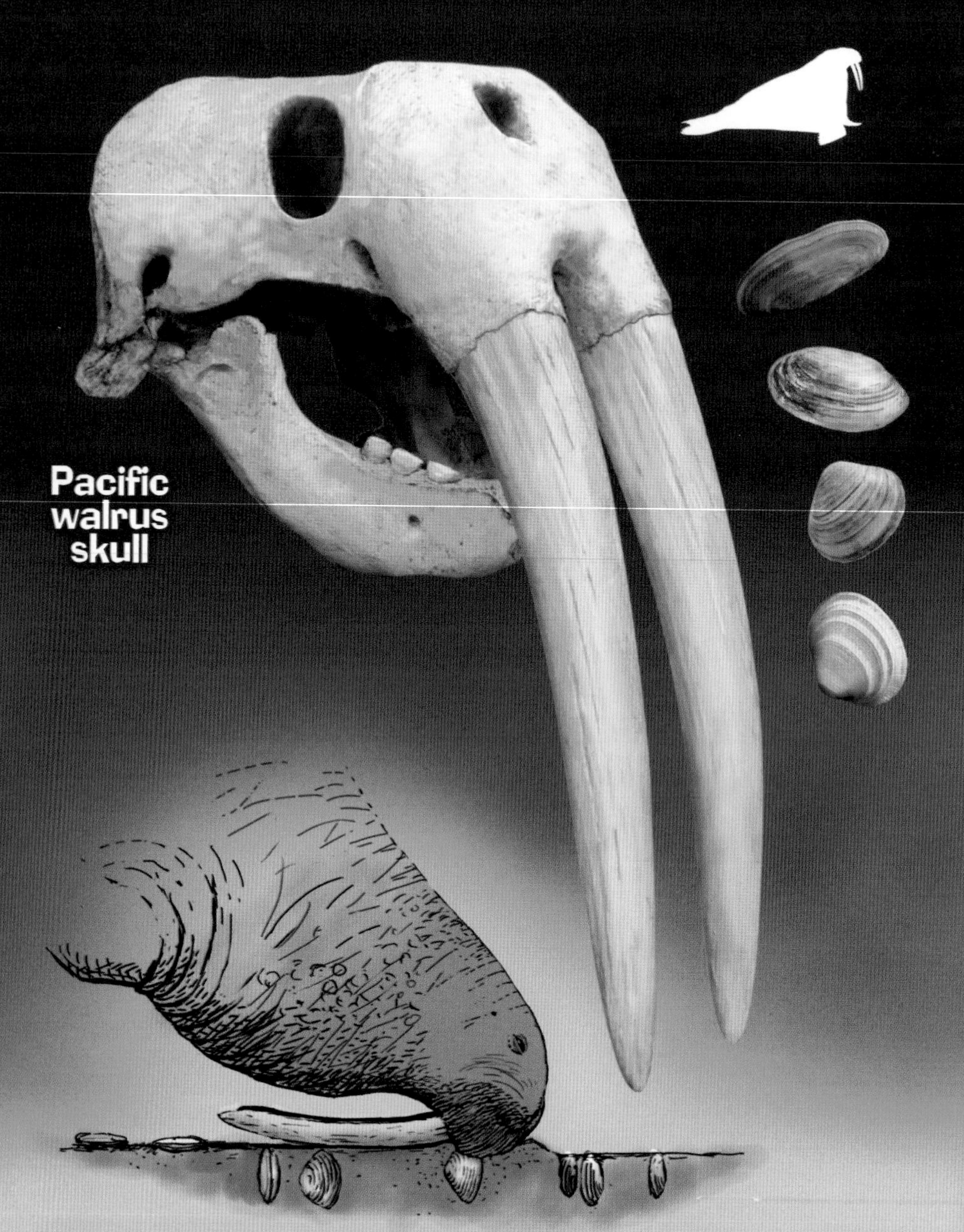

They find clams buried in the sand using their whiskers. A walrus's mouth is designed like a vacuum cleaner to suck the clams out of their shells.

CONTRAST

Here is a southern elephant seal skull. Elephant seals eat fish, squid, sharks, and other seals.

Here is a polar bear skull.

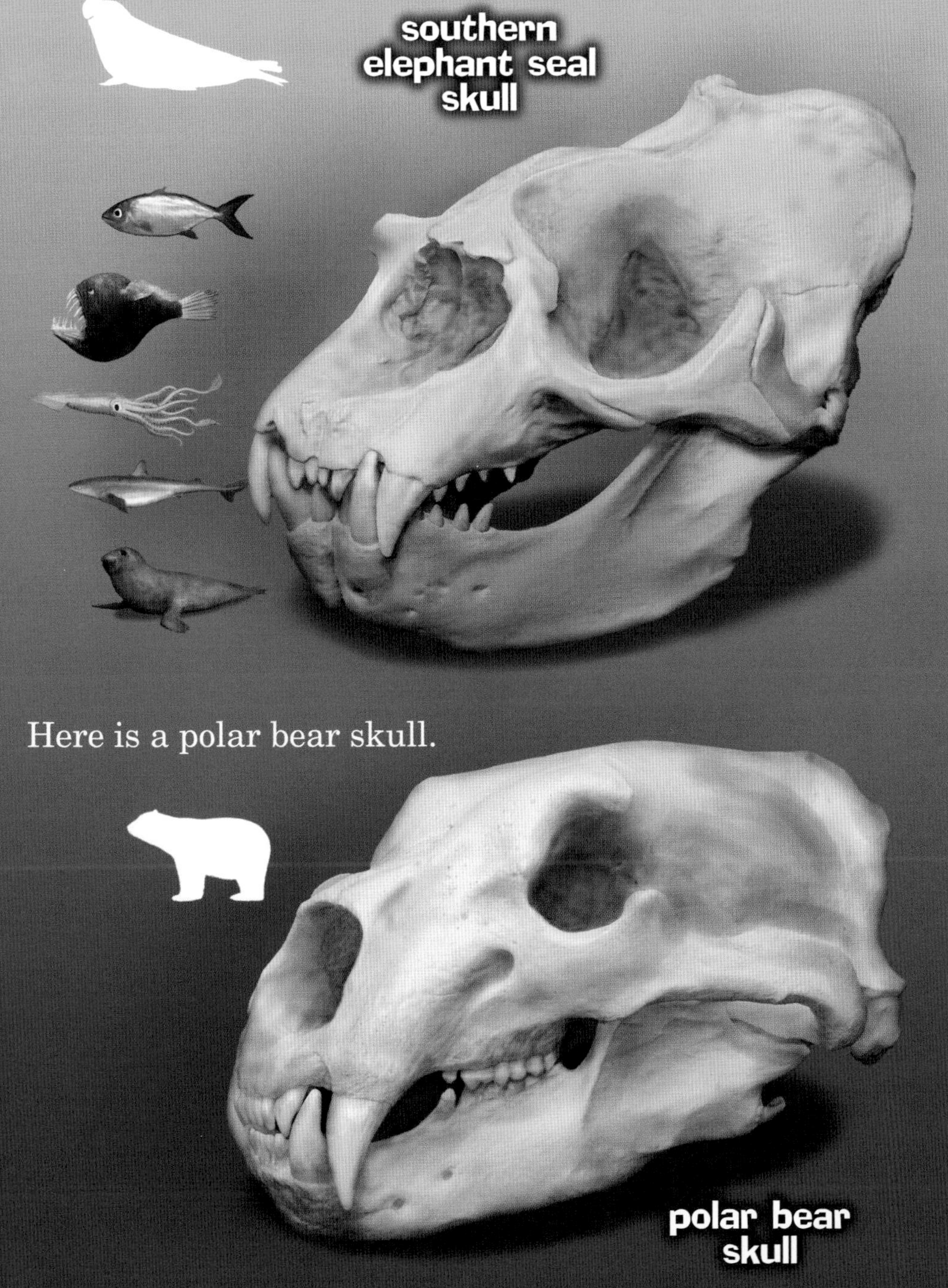

HUDDLE

When walruses want to protect their pups from polar bears, the adults get in a circle and surround their young ones. It is called a huddle of walruses.

GEOGRAPHIC FACT

A walrus has never seen a penguin. A penguin has never seen a polar bear.

SLEEP FACT

Walruses have been known to sleep for up to 19 hours straight.

COLONY

On land, a large group of elephant seals is called a colony. Here is a colony of elephant seals.

LAND FACT

On land, a group of seals could also be called a harem or a rookery.

A large group of seals in the water is called a raft of seals.

DUEL ON LAND

The walrus and the elephant seal are on a beach. They flop, or bounce, while moving. On land they both move more slowly than in water.

The walrus threatens the elephant seal with its long tusks.

The elephant seal is much larger and heavier. It shoves the walrus. The elephant seal is not afraid—it smashes its huge body into the walrus.

It has no trouble pushing the walrus around.

On land, the elephant seal wins.

CLASH ON ICE

Here is a big ice floe. The walrus uses its tusks to pull itself up on the ice. The elephant seal sees the walrus.

DEFINITION
A floe is a sheet of floating ice.

The elephant seal swims around the ice deciding what to do. It tries to climb on the ice floe.

The elephant seal is too heavy to pull itself up on the ice. The walrus uses its tusks to bang the seal's head.

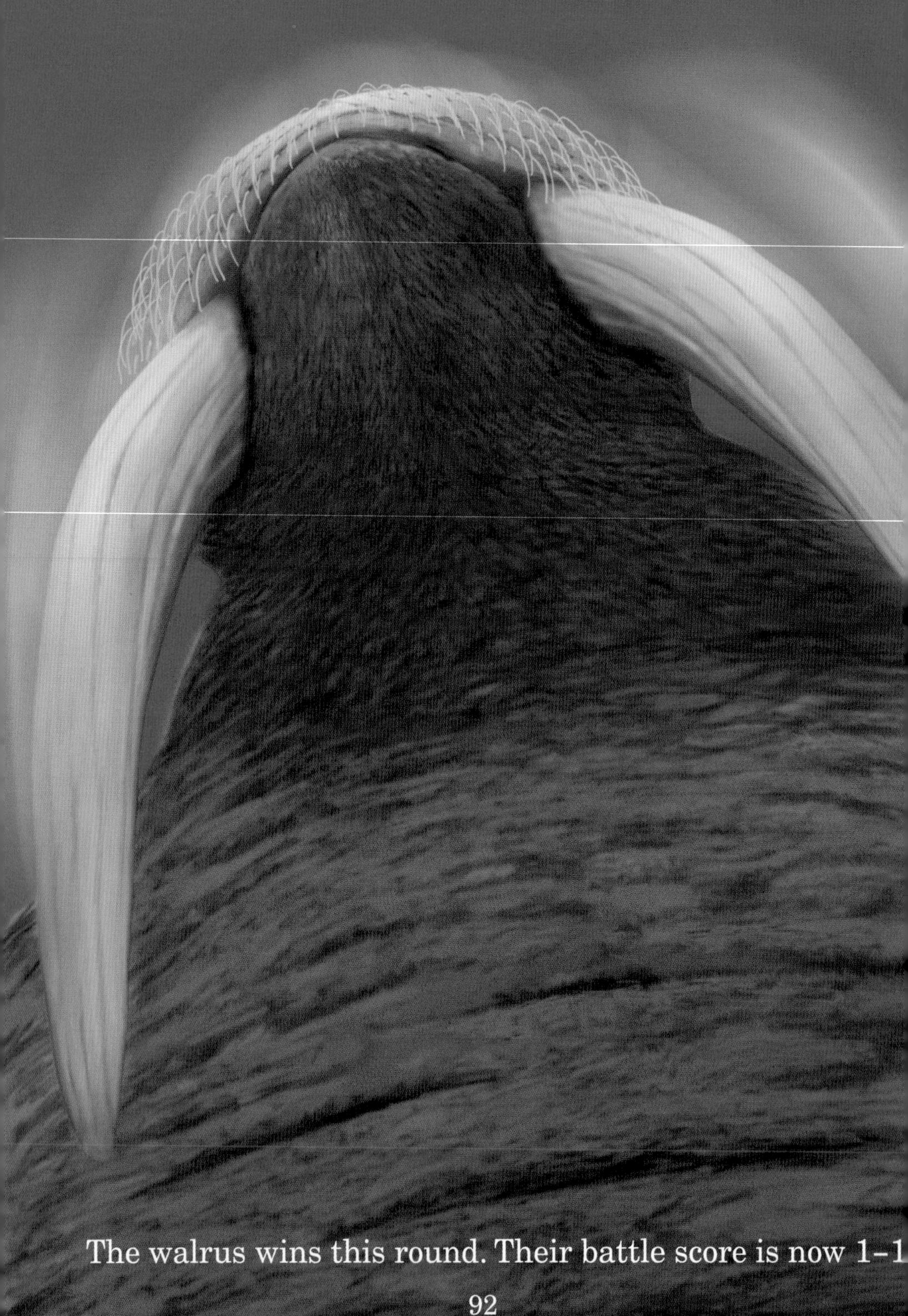

The walrus wins this round. Their battle score is now 1–1

BATTLE IN WATER

In the water the elephant seal has an advantage—it can hold its breath longer than a walrus can. The elephant seal is so heavy it can push the walrus around.

The elephant seal bites the walrus. The walrus has thick skin, but it is wounded. The elephant seal uses its size advantage to push the walrus underwater.

The elephant seal rams the walrus. Boom! Boom! The elephant seal hurts the walrus. The fight is over. The elephant seal has won two of the three battles. Elephant seal wins!

WHO WOULD WIN?®

COYOTE

VS.

DINGO

What would happen if a coyote and a dingo met each other? What if they were both hungry? What if they had a fight? Which one do you think would win?

MEET THE COYOTE

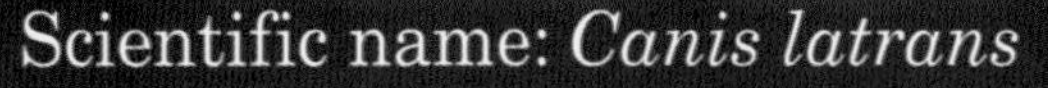

Scientific name: *Canis latrans*

A coyote is a four-legged mammal that looks like a dog. It is a dog! Or is it a wolf? The truth is—it's both!

NAME ORIGIN

The Aztec people named it coyotl, *which eventually became* coyote.

OTHER NAMES

Brush wolf, prairie wolf, and American jackal

Dogs, coyotes, jackals, wolves, and foxes look similar from afar. Coyotes are famous for their howl. AAAAHHHH! Ooooohhhh.

AAAAHHHHOooooohhhh

dog

coyote

jackal

What would happen if a coyote and a dingo met each other? What if they were both hungry? What if they had a fight? Which one do you think would win?

MEET THE COYOTE

Scientific name: *Canis latrans*
A coyote is a four-legged mammal that looks like a dog. It is a dog! Or is it a wolf? The truth is—it's both!

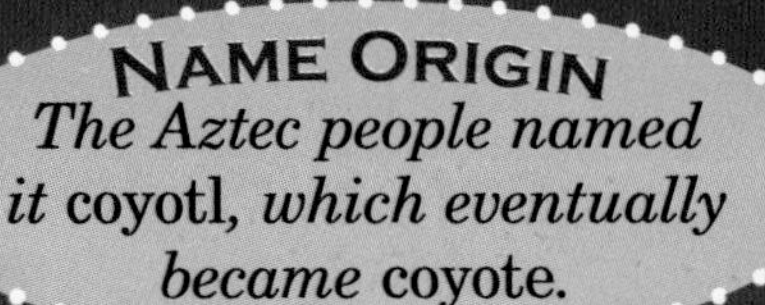

OTHER NAMES
Brush wolf, prairie wolf, and American jackal

Dogs, coyotes, jackals, wolves, and foxes look similar from afar. Coyotes are famous for their howl. AAAAHHHH! Oooooohhhh.

AAAAHHHHOooooohhhh

dog **coyote** **jackal**

MEET THE DINGO

Scientific name: *Canis dingo*

The dingo is known as the apex predator from Down Under. It is the largest land predator in Australia.

NAME ORIGIN
The Aboriginal people of Australia named the dingo.

SLANG
"Down Under" is slang for the continent of Australia.

Dingoes are similar to dogs, coyotes, jackals, wolves, and foxes. Animals in this group are called canines.

NORTH AMERICA

The coyote is from North America. Coyotes are very adaptable. They live in all types of environments: forests, savannas, prairies, brush, deserts, mountains, farmlands, suburbs, and even big cities.

LEGEND
An explorer upon meeting his first coyote said, "It is smart like a fox, shaped like a dog, and ferocious like a wolf."

AUSTRALIA

The dingo is from Australia. The dingo lives in a tough and rugged environment. Australia has a mostly hot and dry climate.

Map

Scientists disagree—is a dingo a wild dog? Or is it more of a wolf?

Here is a coyote next to a mastiff, the heaviest dog on earth. Coyotes are small. They are not as big as their reputations. They weigh about 35 pounds.

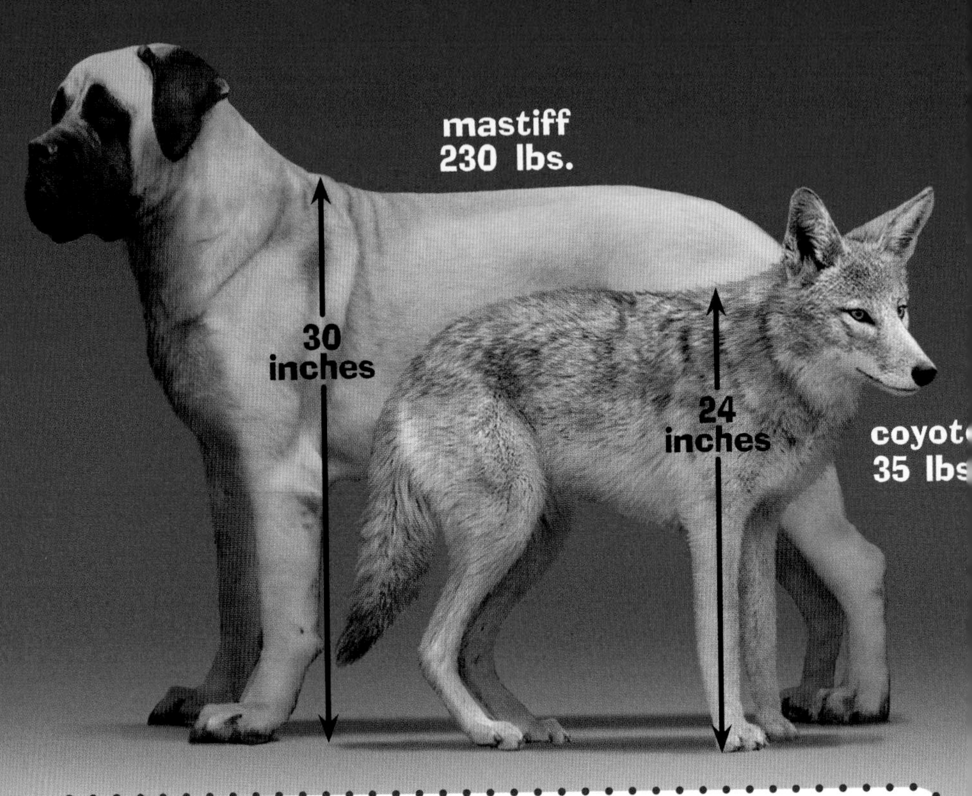

COMPARE
The fastest humans can run at about 27 miles per hour.

SPEED
A coyote can run at 40 miles per hour.

Here is a dingo next to an Irish wolfhound, the tallest dog on Earth.

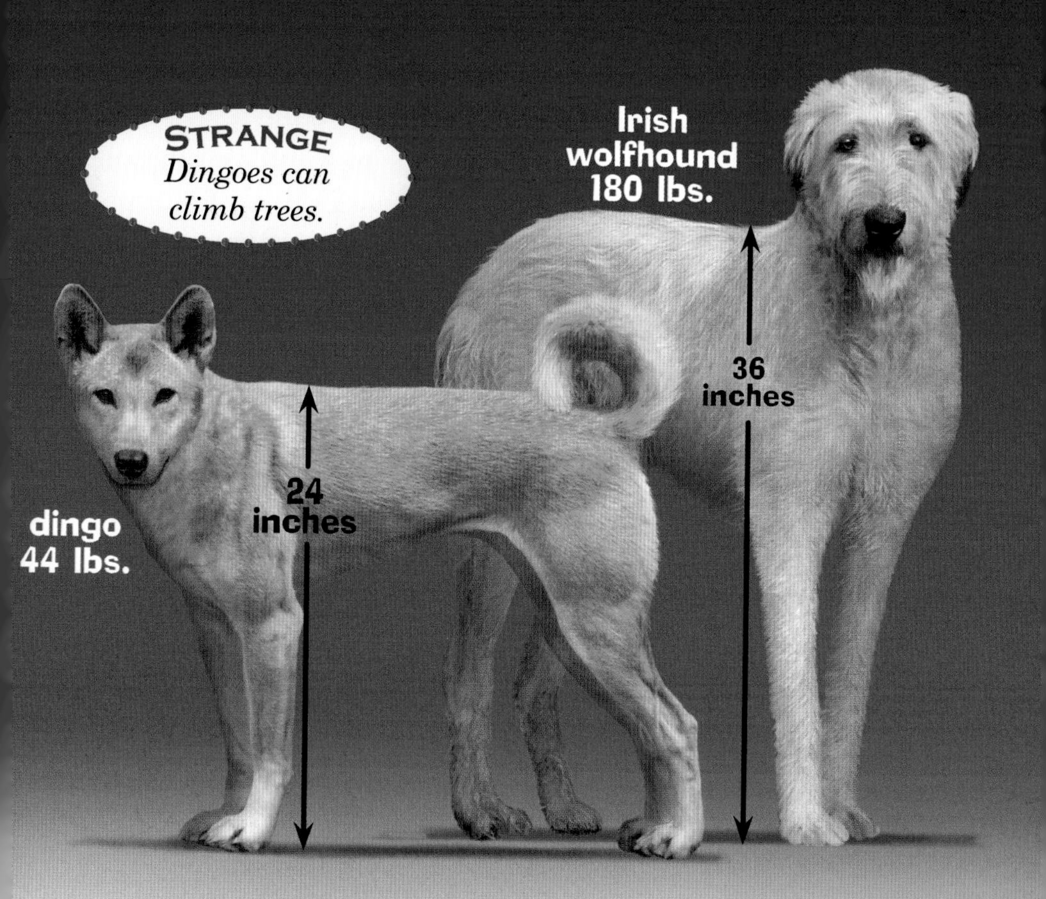

STRANGE
Dingoes can climb trees.

SPEED
A dingo can run about 37 miles per hour. That's faster than a human.

SPEED LIMIT 37

DESCRIBE

Not many wild animals are trained to be pets. The dog is the most domesticated pet on earth. It is often called man's best friend. It is a woman's best friend, too!

DEFINITION
To be domesticated *means to become a pet or live on a farm. Some animals will never be pets.*

This border collie, a farm dog, is protecting a herd of sheep.

DID YOU KNOW?
Wild plants can also be domesticated into food and farmed.

A DOG

Dogs and other canines can be taught tasks and tricks. Dogs do not live as long as most mammals.

FACT

Many people use service dogs, also called seeing eye dogs or guide dogs.

AGING FACT

One dog year is equal to about 7 human years.

DID YOU KNOW?

Dogs sweat from their paws.

HAIR OR FUR?

Mammals have fur or hair. Some have long hair or fur. A coyote has short hair.

Here is a dog with long hair.

GROOMING FACT
Coyotes are usually scruffy-looking.

DID YOU KNOW?
Some dog owners bring their dogs to a dog hairdresser.

Afghan hound

HAIR OR FUR?

A dingo also has short hair.

dingo hair

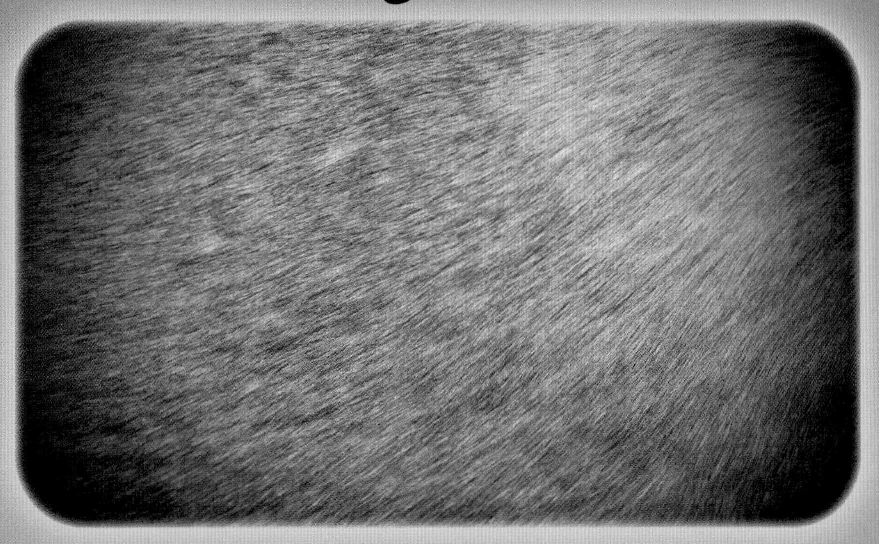

OTHER NAME
A dingo is also called a warrigal.

Here is another dog with long hair!

komondor

POPULAR DOG

Here are some popular dog breeds.

Pekingese

Dalmatian

terrier

Chihuahua

collie

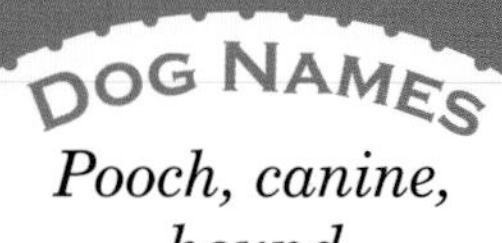

Cavalier

bulldog

chow chow

dachshund

shepherd

BREEDS

Here are more, including some strange dog breeds.

SKELETON

This is a coyote skeleton. It looks exactly like a typical mammal. It has a head, neck, body, ribs, and four legs. It also has a tail.

THAT WAS LOUD!
Coyotes bark, screech, yelp, squeal, and howl!

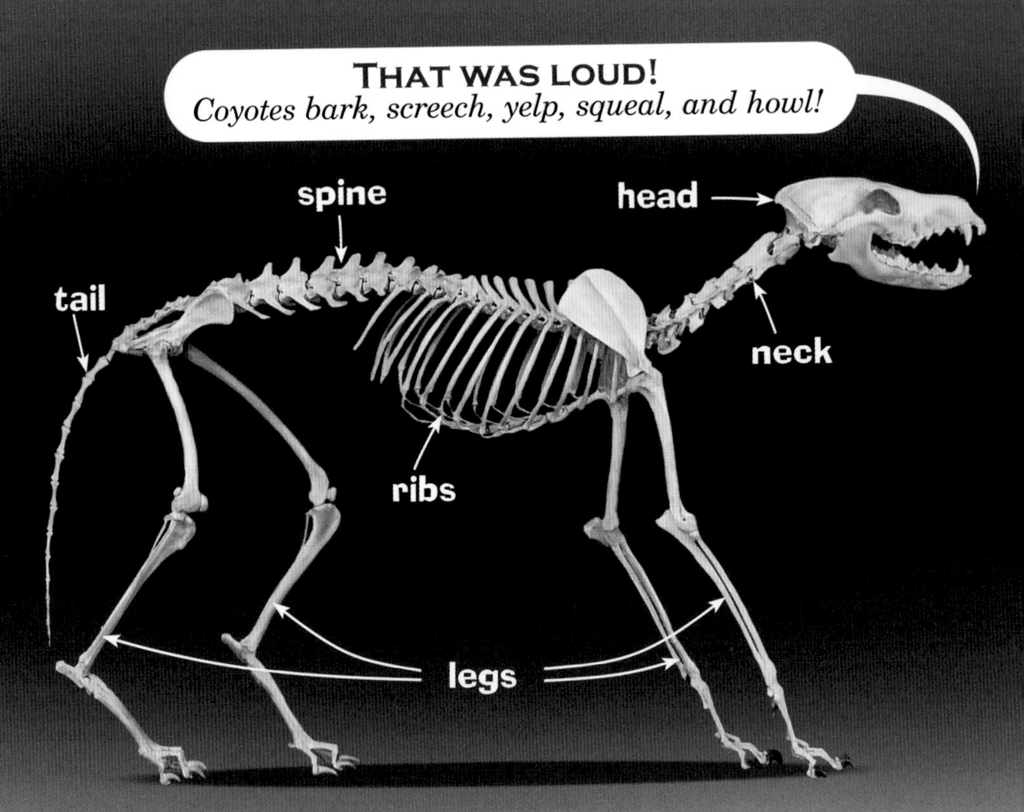

LIGAMENTS VS. TENDONS

Ligaments connect bone to bone. Tendons connect bone to muscle. Cartilage covers the ends of bones, acting like padding.

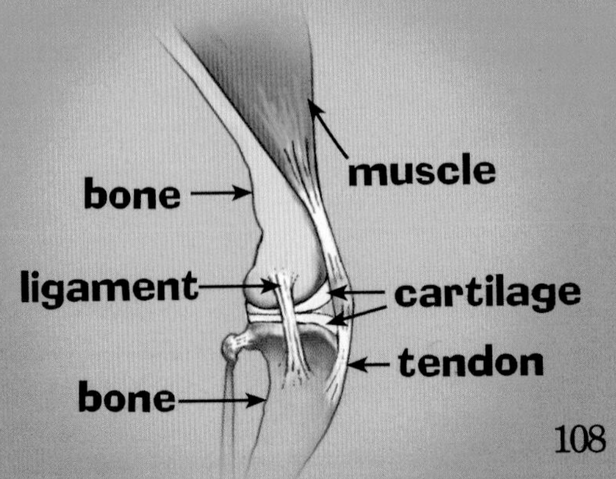

DEFINITION
A skeleton *is the inner bones of an animal.*

ANIMAL PARTS
Ligaments, tendons, muscles, and cartilage are attached to bones.

SKELETON

This is what a dingo skeleton looks like. It is very similar to a coyote skeleton. A dingo can turn its head 180 degrees around. It can stand straight and look behind.

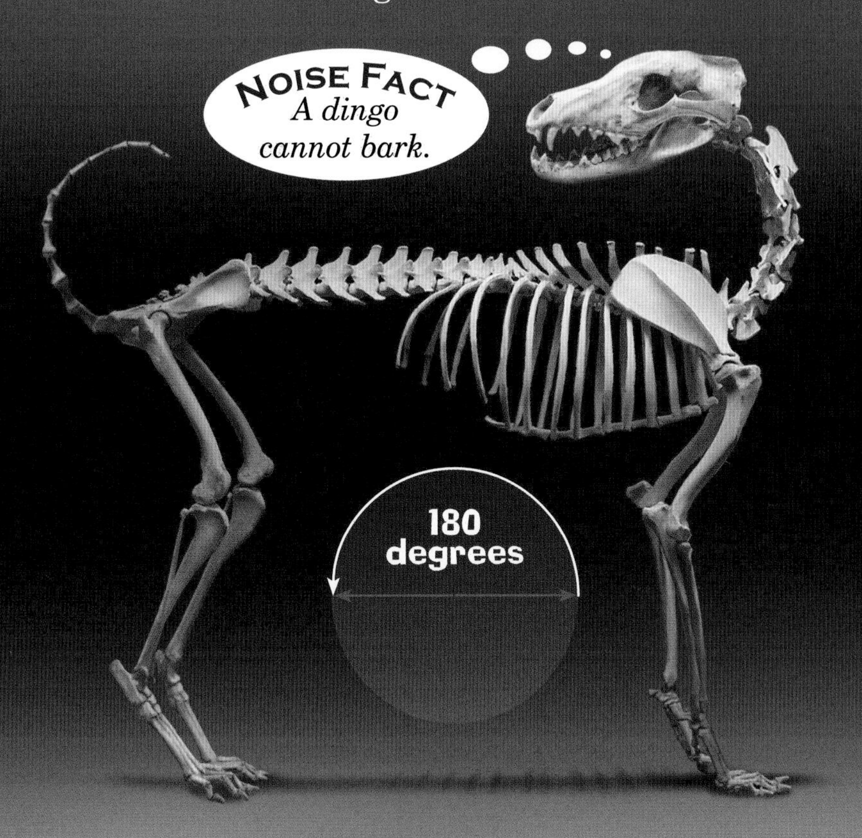

NOISE FACT
A dingo cannot bark.

DANGER!
What could eat a dingo? A saltwater crocodile would have no trouble eating a dingo.

MONEY FACT
Australia has a dingo coin.

Australian 2 oz. Dingo Silver Coin

TEETH

Notice the teeth in a coyote skull. Coyotes and other canines have meat-eating carnivore-type teeth. Their teeth are designed to hold animals, then crack bones and cut meat and tendons.

NEWBORN FACT
A baby canine is called a pup or a puppy.

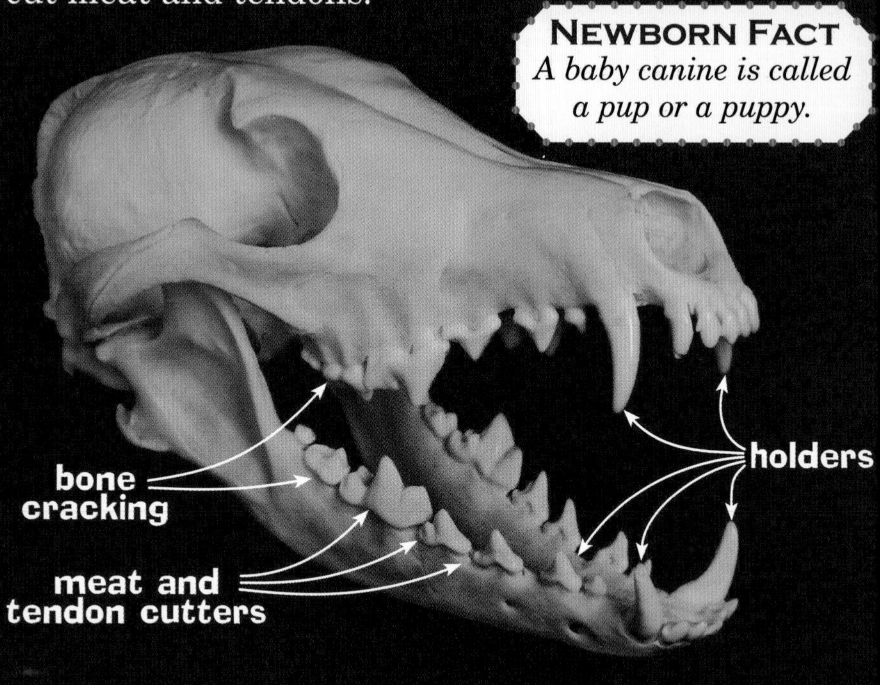

TAIL DOWN

A coyote has a bushy tail. When it runs, its tail is down, not out straight like most dogs.

SIMILAR FACT
A coyote looks very similar to an African black-backed jackal.

SKULL

This is a dingo skull.

PARTS OF THE SKULL

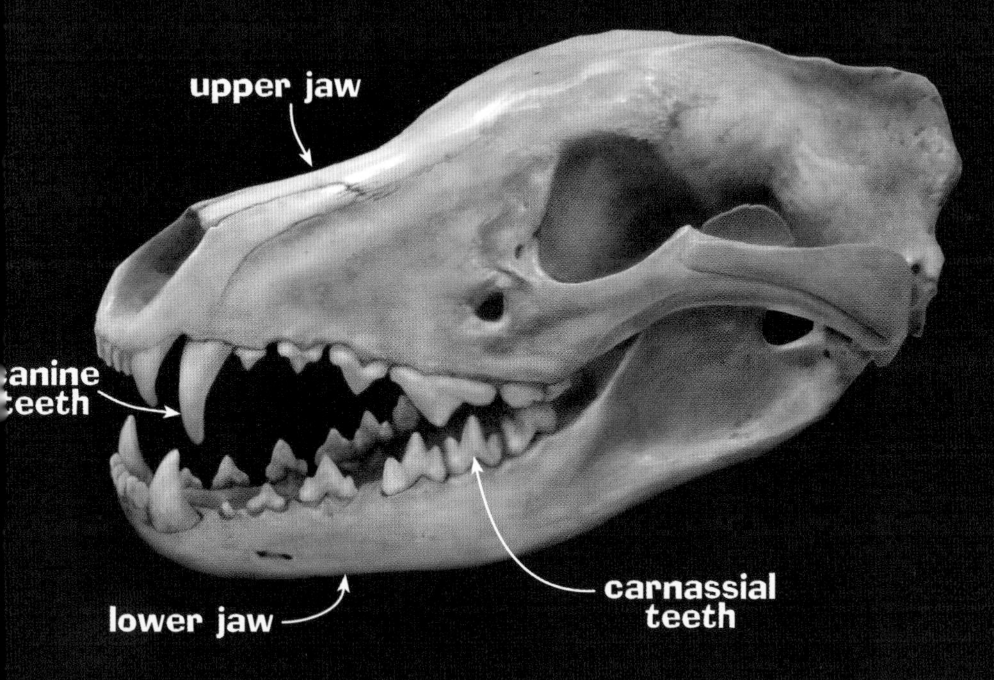

TAIL UP

The dingo tail is bushy. The tail is up flying in the breeze when the dingo is running.

DNA FACT

Scientists have learned that the dingo is related to the New Guinea singing dog.

FOOD

It was thought that coyotes killed cattle, hogs, and other big farm animals.

We now know that coyotes mostly eat small animals like rats, mice, and rabbits.

WARNING!
If you live in coyote territory, keep your small cats and dogs inside at night.

PACK FACT
Coyotes do not hunt in packs

FOOD

Dingoes are the apex mammal predator in Australia. Watch out, wallabies, bunnies, koalas, bandicoots, numbats, and quolls. A dingo will eat you! If you are a big kangaroo or wallaroo, a pack of dingoes will eat you.

APEX FACT
Apex *means "top of the food chain."*

GROUP FACT
Dingoes do hunt in packs.

FOOD FACT
Dingoes also eat reptiles, fish, and birds.

PAWS

This is a coyote footprint. This is a coyote paw. The big print behind the toes is the foot pad.

FOOTPRINT TOE COUNT

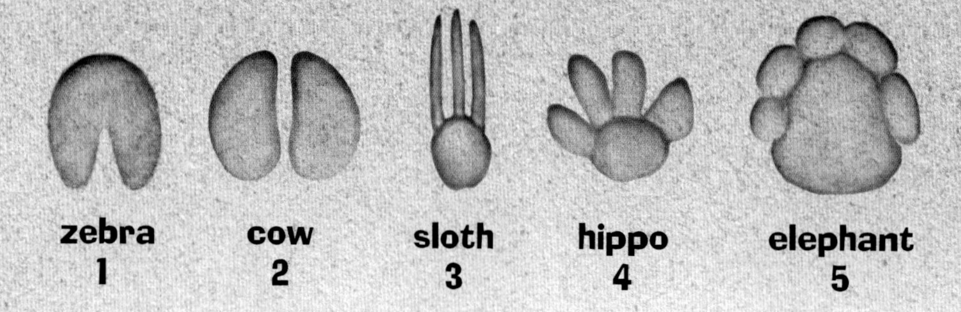

FOOTPRINTS

This is a dingo paw. This is a dingo footprint. Four toes in front, and a foot pad.

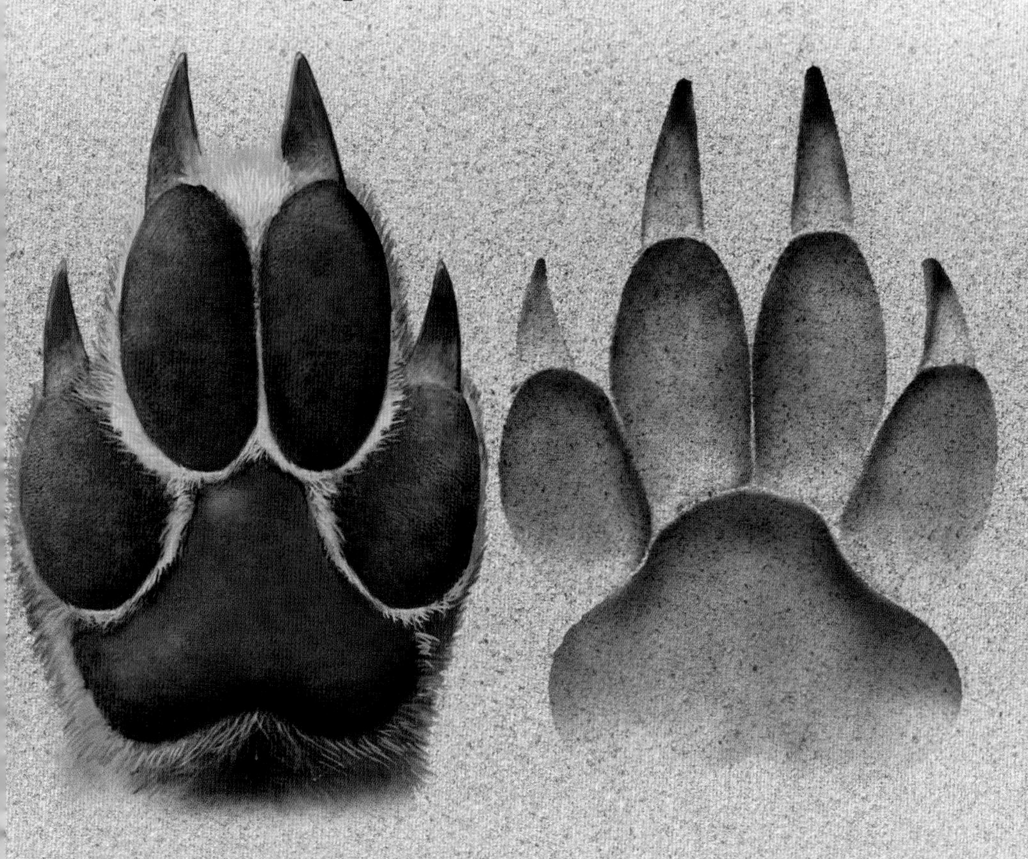

FOOTPRINT TOE COUNT

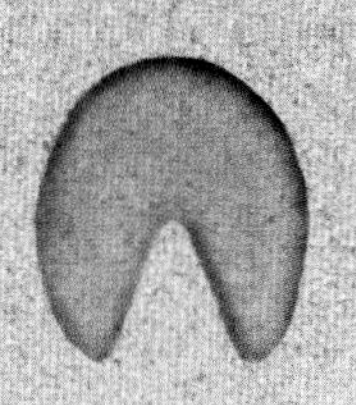

horse
1

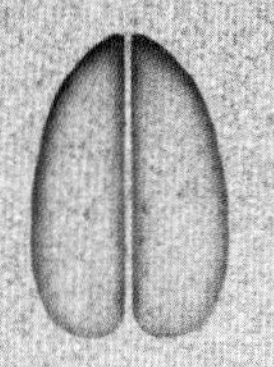

giraffe
2

rhino
3

tapir
4

readers of this book
5

UGLY HISTORY

It is not the coyote's fault, but they have an ugly history. They used to live only out in the western area of North America. Coyotes got blamed by ranchers for missing livestock and poultry.

DEFINITION
Livestock *is cattle, cows, horses, pigs, and goats.*

GOVERNMENT POLICY
The US federal and state governments have been killing coyotes by shooting, poisoning, and trapping. Instead of being wiped out, coyotes are more numerous than ever.

The demise of wolves allowed coyotes to move east into big cities, such as Boston, New York, Philadelphia, Chicago, Atlanta, and Pittsburgh.

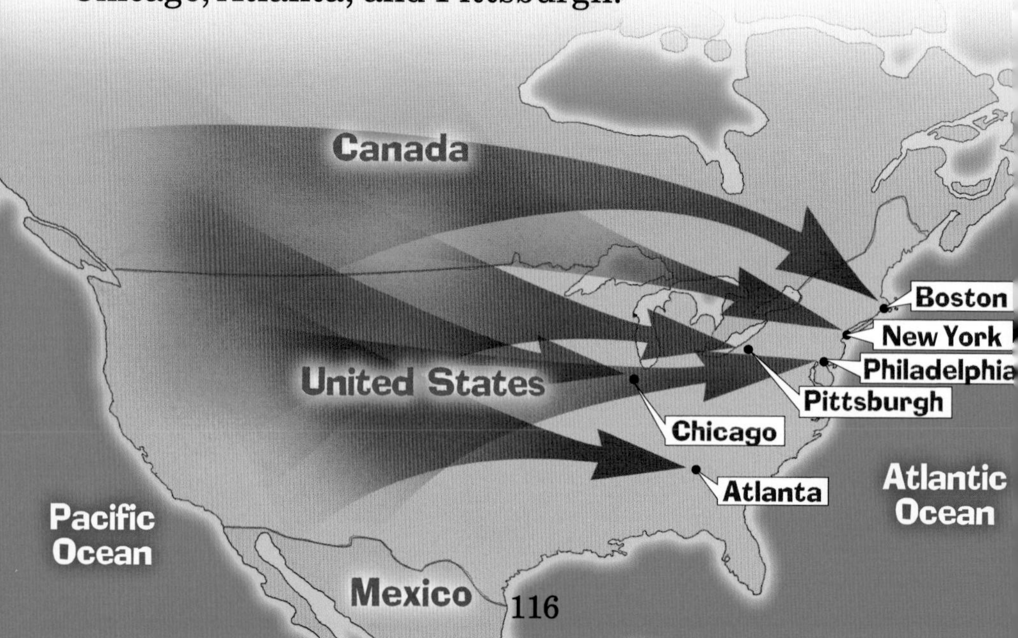

MISUNDERSTOOD

In Australia, dingoes were accused of killing thousands of sheep. They were also accused of killing cattle.

The government of Australia has tried to wipe out the dingo. They even built a 3,000-mile fence. There are dingoes on one side, and no dingoes on the other side.

SNEAKY

WHO TOOK THE FUNNY PAGES?

A coyote was seen riding a train in Portland, Oregon.

CRASH!

A coyote got hit by a car but then hitched a ride 20 miles inside the grill and bumper.

ALL ABOARD!

Coyotes have jumped rides on moving trains.

REPUTATION

LINGO

The way different animals talk. Here's some dingo sign language!

BINGO

A number matching game.

RINGO

A dingo drumming.

FIGHT

It is time for the fight! The coyote tries to trick the dingo. It enters a hollow log and throws up. The smell attracts the dingo to battle, but the coyote has left the area and is hiding in some bushes.

The dingo is not happy. He goes looking for the coyote.

The coyote then sneaks back and hides in the log. The dingo does not see him. Where is that coyote? Come out and fight! After a while, the dingo follows the scent.

He is now face-to-face with the coyote. The coyote outsmarted himself. He is stuck in the log. He can't back up. The coyote has to confront the dingo.

The coyote can't escape. The dingo opens his mouth and bites the coyote in the jaw. Crunch! Ouch!

The coyote has a cut tongue, sore mouth, and broken teeth—he can't fight back. The dingo blocks the opening.

The dingo gives the coyote a few more bites. The ferocious dingo wins and walks away.

WHO HAS THE ADVANTAGE?

CHECKLIST

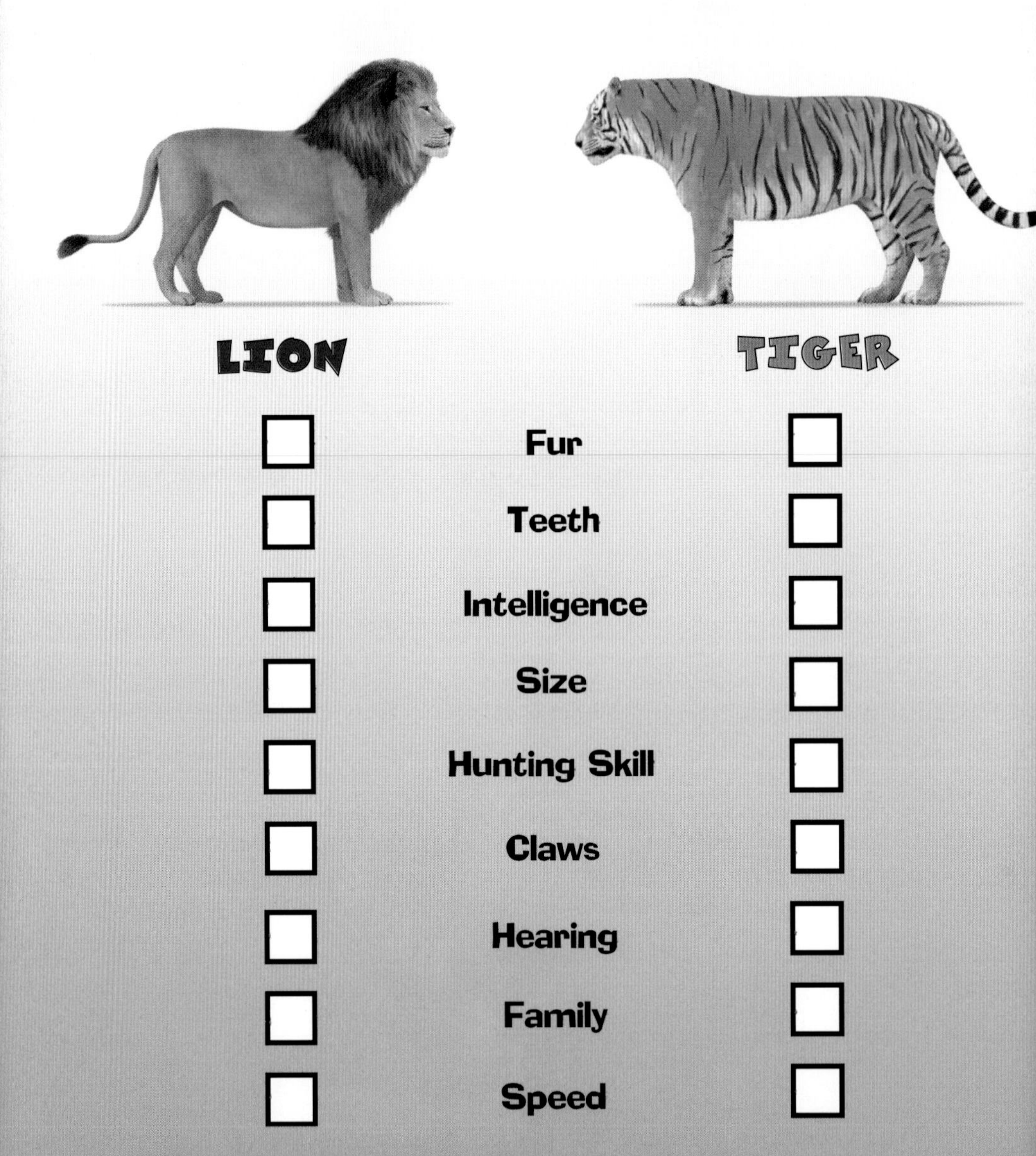

This is one way the fight may have ended. How would you write the ending?

IO HAS THE DVANTAGE?

HECKLIST

NO		HIPPO
☐	Weight	☐
☐	Size	☐
☐	Weapons	☐
☐	Skin	☐
☐	Ears	☐
☐	Swimming ability	☐
☐	Speed	☐

way the fight may have ended.
you write the ending?

WHO HAS THE ADVANTAGE? CHECKLIST

WALRUS		ELEPHANT SEAL
☐	Size	☐
☐	Tusks	☐
☐	Weight	☐
☐	Land Speed	☐
☐	Ocean Speed	☐
☐	Diving	☐
☐	Breath Holding	☐

This is one way the fight may have ended. How would you write the ending?

WHO HAS THE ADVANTAGE? CHECKLIST

COYOTE		DINGO
☐	**Size**	☐
☐	**Speed**	☐
☐	**Eyesight**	☐
☐	**Fur**	☐
☐	**Paws**	☐
☐	**Teeth**	☐

This is one way the fight may have ended. How would you write the ending?

MONSTROUS MAMMALS